Open Knowledge Institutions

Open Knowledge Institutions

Reinventing Universities

Lucy Montgomery, John Hartley, Cameron Neylon, Malcolm Gillies, Eve Gray, Carsten Herrmann-Pillath, Chun-Kai (Karl) Huang, Joan Leach, Jason Potts, Xiang Ren, Katherine Skinner, Cassidy R. Sugimoto, and Katie Wilson

The MIT Press
Cambridge, Massachusetts | London, England

The MIT Press would like to thank the anonymous peer reviewers who provided comments on drafts of this book. The generous work of academic experts is essential for establishing the authority and quality of our publications. We acknowledge with gratitude the contributions of these otherwise uncredited readers.

This book was set in Stone Serif and Stone Sans by Westchester Publishing Services. Printed and bound in the United States of America.

Library of Congress Cataloging-in-Publication Data

Names: Montgomery, Lucy, 1980– author.
Title: Open knowledge institutions : reinventing universities /
    Lucy Montgomery, John Hartley, Cameron Neylon, Malcolm Gillies,
    Eve Gray, Carsten Herrmann-Pillath, Chun-Kai (Karl) Huang, Joan Leach, Jason
    Potts, Xiang Ren, Katherine Skinner, Cassidy R. Sugimoto, Katie Wilson.
Description: Cambridge, Massachusetts : The MIT Press, 2021. |
    Includes bibliographical references and index.
Identifiers: LCCN 2020029454 | ISBN 9780262542432 (paperback)
Subjects: LCSH: Education, Higher--Effect of technological innovations on. |
    Internet in higher education. | Open learning. | MOOCs (Web-based instruction) |
    Universities and colleges--Planning.
Classification: LCC LB2395.7 .M654 2021 | DDC 378.1/7344678--dc23
LC record available at https://lccn.loc.gov/2020029454

10 9 8 7 6 5 4 3 2 1

Contents

Acknowledgments

We would like to thank Curtin University for funding the workshop that has made this book possible. We are especially grateful to Chris Moran, deputy vice-chancellor (research), who took a chance on this novel methodology.

The organizers—Cameron Neylon, Lucy Montgomery, and John Hartley—are eternally grateful to the workshop participants who willingly submitted to twelve-hour days of writing, and brought ideas, energy, and patience to the process. We are also grateful to Emma de Francisco, who provided an extraordinary level of professional and organizational support, without which the workshop—and this book—could not have happened.

We thank Faith Bosworth and Book Sprints (https://www.book sprints.net/) for skilled facilitation, and the courage and diplomacy to wrangle a diverse and opinionated group of scholars into collective productivity. The Book Sprints remote team for the initial publication included Raewyn Whyte (editor), Henrik van Leeuwen (illustrator), Julien Taquet (book production), and Juan Gutierrez (information technology support).

We enjoyed outstanding hospitality at the Moondyne Convention Centre. The excitement that accompanied the release of each day's menu was only matched by the daily encounters with big mobs of kangaroos. Thanks to Chris and Peter Nott.

Finally, the process of converting the output of the Book Sprints into a formally published, open-access scholarly book has been made possible by the vision, commitment, and flexibility of the MIT Press. Our thanks go to Amy Brand, Susan Buckley, and the MIT Press team. They shepherded our manuscript through both an open community peer review process and more traditional closed scholarly review process, and helped to secure the funding needed to make this book available for free under a CC BY license. Our extraordinary privilege in working with this amazing publisher is a reminder of the value of connecting institutions as enablers of open communication.

Preface

The Flight of the Penguin

Allen Lane died in 1970. Shortly before his death, as the founder of Penguin Books, he met with some of Britain's leading academics to propose that a consortium of British universities acquire Penguin Books. Penguin published everything from crime thrillers to Penguin Classics, including Pelican (nonfiction), Peregrine (first editions), Puffin (children's books), and the hardback Allen Lane imprint. By 1970, Penguin was as popular a national institution as the BBC.

Lane's was an early attempt to link two different types of knowledge institutions: popular but serious publishing and learned but modernizing universities. It came to nothing. The university sector at that time was incapable of making use of the popular reach, industrial resources, and global reputation of the firm that had so astoundingly democratized the reading public. The idea of a great publishing venture *as* a university did not accord with universities' self-conception. Indeed, the day after Lane's death, Penguin was sold to another media giant, Pearson; it would later be internationalized as part of Penguin Random House.

In the context of today's debates over control of the systems of scholarly communications and the societal impacts of textbook costs for students, it is clear in hindsight that an opportunity was lost. Universities might have led the transformation of knowledge institutions from closed cloisters to open and globally networked competitors in knowledge services. It took another generation along with the emergence of digital and internet technologies to force that change, eventually making universities an integrated (if specially protected) part of creative, knowledge, and service economies, in which environment they are by no means the dominant players.

In 2012, Pearson withdrew from trade publishing and began the divestiture of Penguin that would be completed by 2017. In January 2018, a distressed Pearson announced yet another cost-cutting venture, including a near-terminal retreat from the field of content production.

So has Lane's dying initiative now come full circle? With universities increasingly focused on funding publishing infrastructures and supporting open educational resources, is there an opportunity to lift the pace in rethinking their embrace of a more open and competitive knowledge role? Could they even be major players in the creative, knowledge, and service economies? What would it take for universities to be ready to take these opportunities in the future?

Introduction

The Moondyne Manifesto

In April 2018, thirteen of us from around Australia and the world gathered, with only the local kangaroos for company, in a secluded venue deep in the Moondyne Valley, an hour or so east of Perth, to think about the future of the university as an open knowledge institution (OKI). This book is the product of that thinking. It represents a consensus view from some distinct perspectives—research professors, open knowledge advocates, science communicators, economists, publishers, high-level university administrators, librarians, and others—toward a diagnosis of what the problem is, and what we might do to fix it.

This book advocates for universities to become OKIs that institutionalize our world's creative diversity in order to contribute to the stock of common knowledge.

Universities operating as OKIs act with principles of openness at their center. We advocate for universities to work with the wider community to generate shared knowledge resources that work for the broader benefit of all humanity. We advocate that universities adopt transparent protocols for the creation, use, and governance of these shared resources.

1

Change

An Open World

In 2016, McKinsey Global Institute released a report on digital globalization that found that data flows across national borders have increased forty-five-fold since 2005 (Manyika et al. 2016). This flow of video, information, searches, communication, transactions, and intracompany traffic now greatly outpaces the movement of people and traded goods. Data globalization has not favored all parts of the world equally, however, with Africa and South America lagging significantly behind the United States, Western Europe, and China in data flow volume. But there can be little doubt that OKIs have a vital role to play in supporting collaboration across national and digital boundaries in a world that is being transformed by new communication possibilities.

As we updated this manuscript in preparation for print publication in early 2020, the COVID-19 pandemic provided a stark reminder of the value of openness, collaboration, and knowledge sharing to global communities as well as the costs of remaining closed. The research and higher education landscape's capacity to support and manage openness quickly became a defining feature of efforts to respond to a truly global health emergency. The threat of COVID-19 to health and economies sparked an unprecedented growth in open access to research outputs. Open science, the practice of making research publications, data sets, and methodologies open, transparent, and accessible, helped to speed the production of new, desperately needed knowledge about COVID-19 (Tingley 2020). The rapid sharing of research data and findings via preprint servers and unprecedented international collaboration allowed fifty-three viral genome sequences to be analyzed and made available by February 2020.

Within a month of the release of the first sequence, the structures of potential drug and antibody targets from the virus were identified and shared with global scientific communities—a process that not long before would have taken years. By the beginning of April 2020, BioRxiv, a site for rapid bioscience communication, had 1,048 reports covering the characteristics, structure, sequence, epidemiology, and treatment of the virus, and more than 12,000 viral genome sequences of hCoV-19 had been shared through the open-access virus database GISAID (Freunde von GISAID e.V. 2020).

In these first months of pandemic response, research was shared more quickly and widely than ever before, reducing the duplication of effort, and enabling infectious disease experts and health system operators to build on expert knowledge immediately. In addition to reducing overall research costs and fostering international collaboration, this approach has saved lives.

The open science approaches deployed in the fight against COVID-19 have been inextricably linked to the processes of experimentation and distributed innovation that began elsewhere on the internet. As such, criticisms, clashes, and identity politics that have accompanied the large-scale shift away from closed processes for verifying expert knowledge, and the careful, mediated approaches to sharing it with wider publics, have also echoed the discord that has arisen when other knowledge-making communities have encountered the darker sides of disintermediation. In spite of their benefits, preprint servers have been criticized as promoting "click-bait science" and subjecting scientific communities to the "tyranny of structurelessness" (Heimstädt 2020).

The politicization of COVID-19's origins, calls to hold China to account for a lack of openness and transparency in sharing information, and demands for legal action against China for the global impacts of the pandemic contributed to the Chinese government's decision to apply restrictions to research into the origins of the novel coronavirus in April 2020 (Henderson et al. 2020; Gan, Hu, and Watson 2020). At the same time, China has insisted on its own efforts to share the science of coronavirus openly. The Chinese ambassador to the United States, Cui Tiankai, said in a webcast, "We are doing our best to have transparency. We are discovering, we are learning. At the same time, we are sharing." He added that "what worries me is indeed lack of transparency, not in terms of science, not in terms of medical treatment, but in terms of some of the political developments, especially here in the United States." Transparency has become a political hot potato globally, with all sides demanding openness but little agreement on what that means (Alper 2020).

While COVID-19 may be the most dramatic recent example of both the hope and challenges associated with open approaches to the production of expert knowledge, the tensions and contradictions at play in this space mirror wider transformations that have been underway for some time. The development of free and open-source software, both as a movement and practical infrastructure, is an instance of another space in which open and networked possibilities have led to incredible innovation as well as new dangers and tensions. The collaborative development of highly specific technical resources in the form of code by people who may have never met physically is perhaps the classic illustration of what is enabled by networked digital communications. The lowered cost of discovery means two (or more) people with a shared interest on opposite sides of the globe can find each other. The massively lowered cost of transferring digital objects means they can contribute to each other's work, and the consequent growth of shared platforms and infrastructures makes that work more widely relevant and usable, reinforcing and growing the network over time.

Networked digital technologies are also creating new potentialities for citizen science and social action. It is now possible for user communities to create upstream change in knowledge production processes in order to ensure downstream benefit. An early innovator in this space was PatientsLikeMe, a citizen science–inspired global patient network and real-time research platform established in 2004, entirely outside the university system, with the goal of creating new sources of data for research on ALS (Lou Gehrig's disease), and ultimately speeding the pace of treatment and drug development taking place within the formal research sector. In 2011, the platform expanded beyond ALS, "welcoming any person living with any condition to connect with others, learn and take control of their health." In 2019, PatientsLikeMe became part of the UnitedHealth Group's Research and Development Unit. PatientsLikeMe (2020) now has more than 750,000 members worldwide and has become "the world's largest personalised health network." Data contributed by patient communities have been used to support new clinical trials, and patient-reported information is being connected with biological data at unprecedented scale, allowing the development of more nuanced, and patient-centered approaches to understanding diseases.

At the same time, many digitally enabled "open" projects are facing crises of discrimination, particularly around such identity-based facets as gender, race, and ethnicity. Again, open-source software development provides a striking example of this challenge. In open source, networks are built based on shared technical needs and interests. This reinforces the connections between a subset of global populations with early access to networks: predominantly white men in a small subset of geographies. Early work to enhance diversity within open-source software communities was not pursued. As a result, as our model predicts, these spaces have continued a slide toward a closed state in which participants from other demographics are treated with anger, aggression, and hostility, as evident in the Gamergate movement (Aghazadeh et al. 2018).

Similar stories could be told about Wikipedia (2020a, 2020b) and many other projects that stand out as successes in the creation of OKIs, but that have serious and systemic problems of closed and exclusionary cultures. Learning from these examples, many new projects are expending significant effort to create strong governance structures that address a spectrum of "open" characteristics wherein participants agree to bind themselves to codes of conduct and other processes. These deliberately impose an ongoing burden of thoughtfulness and labor to ensure that the system is optimized for maximal openness.

Open Initiatives in Universities

Understanding the future of this trend and what it means for knowledge institutions is not straightforward. Global data on data flows do not equate to or even map onto global knowledge. A specific narrative about the successful mediation of knowledge in one setting cannot necessarily be generalized, and the growth of open-access policy, platform provision, and outcomes is only a narrow slice of a broader picture. But there are some indications that universities on the road to being successful OKIs can be positioned to engage more productively with these shifts.

Universities in North America, Europe, Australia, and Aotearoa New Zealand have already experienced major changes in knowledge format and accessibility as a result of digital technologies. Since the 1990s, scholarly resources in many disciplines (though not all) have

Case Study 1
Wikipedia

Wikipedia provides a good example of an open knowledge platform called to account for its embedded gender, ethnic, and racial bias in the creation and sharing of public knowledge. As it became an influential and highly popular free online encyclopedia developed largely by technology-savvy volunteers, the impact of implicit assumptions in some Wikipedia contributions became apparent.

Wikipedia attracted criticism for systemic bias on the basis of gender, race, language, and culture relating to both the topics that are covered by the free online encyclopedia and ways in which contributions are edited. Criticisms of bias began to emerge as early as 2007, but media coverage of the problem took until 2011 to appear (Lam et al. 2011; Tsvetkova et al. 2017). Critiques of Wikipedia's tendency toward biased, exclusionary practices exposed a culture of volunteer Wikipedia editors who were primarily male, white, English speaking, and from the Global North. Sue Gardner (2011), the former Wikimedia Foundation executive director, summarized comments from women providing reasons why they were discouraged from editing, noting that some women experienced persistent overriding of their decisions by male editors who reverted their editing decisions, and removed suggestions or entries they had contributed. Shyong Lam and colleagues (2011, 9) found female contributors were "being reverted disproportionately" and encountered more adversity. This behavior continued in some of the "edit-a-thons" implemented in the hope of fostering a wider range of Wikipedia editors. A further issue has been the underrepresentation of women and people of color as a focus of Wikipedia entries. In order for a biographical entry about a person to be included on Wikipedia, the platform's guidelines require a person to be "notable." Decisions about whether an individual qualifies as notable are inevitably subjective, and prone to implicit gender and racial bias (Boboltz 2015). The status of biographies of notable women continues to be a battleground, with women scientists' biographical entries being challenged and removed from Wikipedia by editors in 2018 and 2019, before being reinstated, such as in the case of physicist and Nobel Prize winner Donna Strickland, astrophysicist Sarah Tuttle, and nuclear chemist Clarice Phelps (Krämer 2019). All three Wikipedia pages existed at the time of this writing.

In response to gender and race coverage criticisms, the Wikimedia Foundation and US National Science Foundation have provided funding to increase the diversity of Wikipedia as well as improve coverage of content and topics from the Global South. WikiProjects promoting perspectives on gender that extend beyond the gender binary have been established (Wikipedia 2020a, 2020b). Efforts have also been made to address Wikipedia's racial bias, including its limited coverage of Black history in the United States as well as minority peoples, cultures, and languages. As of August 2020, Wikipedia articles had been created in 313 languages, with 303 active and 10 closed (Wikipedia 2020c).

The question of the nature and impact of Wikipedia editing is complicated by the fact that editing is shared by human editors and bots or automated editors. In 2014, bots undertook about 15 percent of the editing, but the extent and editing behaviors of bots vary across Wikipedia's language editions. Bots sometimes revert each other's edits, and can be as unpredictable and inefficient as human editors. For smaller-language versions of Wikipedia, bots edit up to 50 percent or more of the content (Tsvetkova et al. 2017). Bots may be more balanced in their editing than human editors, but they are designed, created, and run by humans, and thus carry cultural and social biases. This case study of Wikipedia exemplifies the challenges of ensuring diversity and openness in knowledge, and the importance of and need for constant monitoring to ensure governance structures and policies respond equitably.

become increasingly available online, with libraries choosing electronic media as a preference. One outcome has been the widening of access to published scholarly materials beyond the physical structures and opening hours of university libraries. This flexibility has proven invaluable in the wake of COVID-19 as universities around the world have scrambled to make courses available to students, even as campuses have been closed and face-to-face teaching has been placed on hold. Less welcome outcomes for many include the shift from "owned" to "rented" collections whereby electronic content has largely been subscribed to rather than purchased, limiting its permanence; the paywalls and increased restrictions based on the licensing of this content; and the closing and shrinking of library buildings and communities of space (Wilson et al. 2019). The costs and management of storage space and demand for student technology study facilities are converging, prompting many libraries to move physical collections off-site or remove items altogether. Particularly in the humanities and creative arts, losing physical access to archives and collections challenges established research practices.

If properly poised, however, open practices could help to broaden as opposed to reduce access to electronic content. Work within university libraries, often in partnership with university presses, is demonstrating how to reclaim the modes of scholarly production through the creation of open journals, open monographs, open data sets, and new curatorial and exhibitionary practices (Library Publishing Coalition 2020). Without such activities to counter the increased commodification of knowledge objects, access to publicly funded library knowledge resources and physical facilities will be much more controlled and restricted than in past decades, thereby limiting openness.

In addition, universities today produce a wide range of openly available materials and rely on open-source software to distribute them. From well-established pathways with large user bases and broad recognition (e.g., arXiv, Sakai, EPrints, and Samvera) to newer, still-experimental environments with great promise (e.g., the integrative, collaborative scholarly publishing platform Manifold), many aspects of "open" are already accepted, if not prominent in the university landscape. When universities trust that openness will increase the reach of their scholarship without compromising (or being perceived as compromising) its value, they are more likely to begin moving toward the characteristics of an OKI.

Universities are expending significant resources and work in grappling with these changes. Normally this happens within a background of existing power, prestige, resources, and practice. While much of the impetus has been driven by outside forces, including funders as well as national and regional policies, we do see specific universities and other research organizations choosing to take a leadership position on these issues, particularly when that openness demonstrates an increase in the return on investment on research or a pathway to lowering the overall costs of scholarly communications. While policy statements and submissions to external assessments do not provide direct evidence of action or outcomes, they have been the catalyst for progress. This can be seen in the case of open access, but also in larger diversity issues, such as the Athena SWAN Charter in the United Kingdom that seeks to advance gender equality in science, technology, engineering, mathematics, and medicine (STEMM).

Case Study 2
The Library Publishing Coalition

The Library Publishing Coalition is an international coalition of libraries and library consortia committed to the vision of "a scholarly communication landscape that is open, inclusive and sustainable." Established in 2013 with an initial membership of sixty-one academic libraries, the coalition now includes more than ninety predominantly North American institutions. The coalition was created in response to the need for a central space in which the growing number of libraries actively involved in publishing "can meet, work together, share information and confront common issues" (Library Publishing Coalition 2020).

Both the establishment and success of the Library Publishing Coalition reflect the active role that many libraries are playing in the processes of experimentation, innovation, and collaboration needed to create as well as support OKIs. Members of the Library Publishing Coalition are proactively filling gaps in established scholarly communication landscapes by establishing their own open-access publishing operations. They are providing scholars with opportunities to publish open-access monographs, journals, and data sets, and collaborating with research funders, researchers, and established publishers to develop new tools, and explore the possibilities for connecting research with communities in rich, meaningful, and open ways (Schlosser 2018). The Library Publishing Coalition demonstrates that libraries are responding to the new opportunities and challenges associated with digital technologies in ways that are far from passive.

There is increasing proof that engaging with an open agenda is good for universities. Caroline Wagner and Koen Jonkers have presented evidence that countries with greater openness have stronger science. They say that there is "a clear correlation between a nation's scientific influence and the links it fosters with foreign researchers" (Wagner and Jonkers 2017). In complementary work, Cassidy Sugimoto and colleagues (2017) demonstrated that institutionally mobile researchers have greater research impact. These studies show the potential benefits to universities of greater openness on traditionally valued measures of performance, but also illustrate the risks of a focus on those traditional measures, derived from limited sets of publications and limited metrics with known and serious biases.

Open institutions bring "data shadows" into the light, thus creating more data and potentially more knowledge. The exponential increase in the flow of data is not uniform, however; it is dominated by transatlantic, European, and Asian streams with much lower rates of flow among African and South American streams and countries of the Global South. This demonstrates the ways in which this flow is globalized but not at all global, and highlights the question of missing and unavailable data as well as the unequal distribution of both data and knowledge around the world. Redressing these asymmetries is clearly part of the agenda of future-facing OKIs, not least because doing so would expand the overall knowledge universe enormously, and further diversify its forms, agents, and uses, to the benefit of all.

We can see at least the beginning of institutions looking to gain advantage not by exclusive access to information but rather by the strategic engagement of their data and researchers with others. OKIs will have the capacity to take the available data in massive global data flows and translate them into knowledge. Those flows may travel without regard to local conditions, but open institutions can take transmitted data and translate them into usable and meaningful knowledge, sharing it among groups that might otherwise resist the external incursion of ideas. The potential for global knowledge growth with networked open institutions is great, but networks cannot be uniform across all demographic and national borders. Data must adapt to the given cultural environment, as organizations and people do, and information must be made meaningful if it is to be used for transforming knowledge.

Open Knowledge and Conflict

OKIs cultivate cross-border exchange. A diversity of perspectives and experiences is critical for increasing the value of a knowledge-producing network. This requires work, and these efforts are often challenging, with increasing difference inevitably leading to conflict. Our world feels ever-more hemmed in by resurgent cross-border conflict among nations, faith groups, class, gender and ethnic groups, and extremism on the Right and Left, all the way across to differences of identity, affiliation, and taste that divide people even as they connect. We can be confident that the current era of globalization in trade, technology, and media—not to mention a few supranational languages (led by Mandarin, Spanish, English, and Arabic)—will not lead to cultural or knowledge uniformity.

The friction created by cross-border conflict can be a driver and catalyst for knowledge. These borderlands provide the most intensive zones of knowledge exchange and competition, bringing previously separate ideas into contact to offer innovative solutions to previously unimagined threats and opportunities. An OKI will be an environment where difference and conflict are always visible, and untranslatable, incommensurable, and incomprehensible knowledge will be a deliberately cultivated part of the landscape. The institutional imperative is to maintain contact across such borders rather than closing them down or seeking to incorporate them into some larger, smoother entity.

Conflict is already woven into the mechanisms and core cultural practices of the university. Peer review is perhaps the most obvious example, as a stage in which authors and referees engage in conflict to test the claims of a scholarly output in a defined arena with highly specified rules imposed by an editor. The method of producing new academics also engages in a discourse of conflict—notably the tradition of a dissertation "defense" where external examiners are engaged as "opponents" to bring different perspectives to challenge doctoral work.

Extending conflict and diversity in an OKI is not without challenges. Look, for instance, at the "creative destruction," to use Joseph Schumpeter's term (McCraw 2007), of the once-mighty empires of the press, print publishing, and journalism. Already, many great mastheads have disappeared. There are survivors and standouts, but upheaval in the publishing sector already has led to transformed business plans, contents, workforces, and demographics of attention. There are few outlets left online or off-line that reach for population-wide undifferentiated readerships as did the old "mass media," speaking equally to political leaders, business interests, and working families. Now, online communication is propelled by either advertising (in which case content is free), or subscription (in which case audiences are niche). Knowledge making in this sphere is an entirely new game, driven primarily by the tech giants rather than the journalists and media moguls of the past.

A successful OKI will be modular in its external and internal networks. All nodes will not be equal and open to all others. Some will be closed internally, even while connected externally to other nodes and the rest of the system. The chances of getting it wrong are high, and doing so can be catastrophic not simply for an individual organization but an entire sector. It is quite possible that getting the open knowledge institutional settings wrong for long enough, across a sufficiently significant proportion of the sector, will lead the entire species toward an extinction event: universities will be outcompeted and rendered unfit for purpose. The effort required to maintain a dynamic equilibrium, a poised institutional state, requires continuous challenge and work.

Open by Design

The important policy implication for OKIs is that dystopia looms at both extremes: too open leads to chaos, and too closed leads to rigidity. The possibility space for achieving a poised system is quite narrow. We have presented what is in many ways a utopian vision, and contrasted it with the dystopia of top-down control or, worse, failure of the university as a societal institution. In much contemporary

---

Case Study 3
Activism and the Tyranny of Structurelessness

Although we tend to think of institutions as marble-clad edifices, it is also the case that social movements develop institutional form as they become established in action and across demographics, often in conflict with and struggle against existing institutions (Felski 1989). Protest movements take this path, frequently needing careful internal work to create and maintain dynamic equilibrium, even as they seek to provoke change in the wider social system. An example of one such institution is feminism, which has gone through several evolutionary stages (second- and third-wave feminism, for instance). When second-wave feminism was at its most insurrectionary and militant, in the 1960s and 1970s, activists commonly rejected the imposition of institutional rules and structures on the movement. Yet this led to what Jo Freeman, in a famous 1970 pamphlet, identified as "the tyranny of structurelessness," showing how the lack of structure jeopardized collective decision making and activism, and thus the movement itself. As Freeman (n.d.) wrote,

> If the movement is to move beyond these elementary stages of development, it will have to disabuse itself of some of its prejudices about organization and structure. There is nothing inherently bad about either of these. They can be and often are misused, but to reject them out of hand because they are misused is to deny ourselves the necessary tools to further development. We need to understand why "structurelessness" does not work.

We can learn from this that openness does not entail or necessitate structurelessness, nor can institutions avoid the rule-making process. Freeman recommended reflexivity, such that the process by which openness is achieved is made explicit in organizational routines, especially where there is internal conflict or debate.

---

literature, that dystopia is presented as total corporate control of the academy, or if not that, then the loss of the university's qualities to the pursuit of metricized rankings of excellence (Donoghue 2008; Readings 1996). But there is equally a dystopia in which there is too much freedom—a data deluge or information overload in which anything goes, and no knowledge is more valid than any other.

All institutions are arrayed on a spectrum between order and chaos, between the costs of disorder and the costs of dictatorship (Hartley, Wen, and Li 2015, 176–179). Somewhere on that gradient is a dynamic optimum (figure 1.1), a complex state poised between total control (rigidity) and chaos (collapse), where the system displays desirable qualities of resilience, adaptability, and dynamic efficiency because it has enough flexibility to change and enough structure to remain stable.

The space for policy is not at the extremes but rather in the narrow zone of uncertainty where the pressures of order and disorder can be "poised." "Networks on the boundary between order and chaos may have the flexibility to adapt rapidly and successfully through the accumulation of useful variations. . . . Poised systems will . . . typically adapt to a changing environment gradually, but if necessary, they can occasionally change rapidly. These properties are observed in organisms" (Kauffman 1991).

All institutions can be arrayed about the institutional possibility frontier (figure 1.2) as a trade-off between social costs of disorder and dictatorship (see Djankov et al. 2003).

The nature of this "optimal institutional zone" means it is not something that can be defined in advance but instead must be found through search, with some inevitable trial and error involved. A successful system manages this process and tension continuously. Some degree of organization is required, but flexibility is also necessary for the system to thrive. In the same way, open markets, open competition, and personal freedom still require regulation, both formal via rule of law and social via informal sanctions, to keep the playing field level for cooperating players, discourage free riders, assist disadvantaged or developing groups, and train new entrants

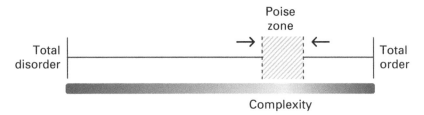

Figure 1.1
Openness as a poised system.

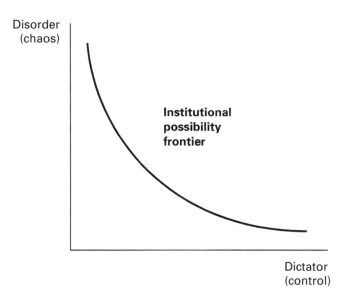

Figure 1.2
Institutional possibility frontier for open knowledge.

into the system. But overregulation, prohibitions, private deals (corruption), and the arbitrary or capricious exercise of power all damage the workings of the system as a whole.

A good example of this is Creative Commons licenses. These licenses use the existing copyright framework (the environment) to allow the selection of an optimal position between retaining complete control over content (all rights reserved or in the extreme form secrecy) and completely giving up control. A user selects a limited set of restrictions, some rights reserved, that they feel are appropriate to their circumstances (Creative Commons 2019a). Yet the use and indeed legal text of the licenses has changed over time in continuous response to newly discovered issues and challenges. The institution of Creative Commons is as much that process of improvement and testing as it is a set of licenses.

Productivity requires balance among alternative and often contending pressures. Different systems, phases, and regimes experience (or

Case Study 4
Creative Commons International License Porting Project

Creative Commons (2019b) is a US-based nonprofit organization (NGO) "dedicated to building a globally-accessible public commons of knowledge and culture." Lowering the transaction costs associated with copyright in digitally enabled, global creative landscapes as well as countering the freezing effects of a copyright system that requires author permission for the reuse, sharing, and adaptation of creative works is the heart of the Creative Commons project. Creative Commons licenses do this by helping creators, authors, and content producers to ensure that license information travels with a creative work as it moves through the digital landscape, clearly communicating information about rights that an author or creator has reserved along with those that have been waived to downstream users.

In 2002, Creative Commons released its first, free-to-use copyright licenses. Although the licenses were drafted in accordance with US copyright law, they were enthusiastically adopted by creative communities in other jurisdictions. Global interest prompted discussions about the need for national versions of the licenses and the establishment of Creative Commons International in 2003. Creative Commons International oversaw porting of the core Creative Commons licenses for use in different national copyright legislatures. This included translating the licenses into local languages as well as ensuring that the licenses were legally translated, adapted, and enforceable within local jurisdictions (Maracke 2010).

Creative Commons licenses have now become a key global standard for the sharing and reuse of content internationally. By 2017, more than 1.4 billion Creative Commons (2017) licensed works had been shared online, including via platforms such as YouTube, Wikipedia, Flickr, and PLOS. The mobilization and continued involvement of a community of technical and legal experts, advocates, educators, and scientists has been key to the movement's success. By 2020, Creative Commons Global Network (n.d.) had chapters in forty-three countries around the world. Continued processes of legal translation, commentary, and critique, the development of scholarship and activism focused on Creative Commons, and technical collaboration have resulted in a vibrant and responsive global movement, rather than a simple legal or technological "fix."

This process of community building and internationalization came full circle with the release of the fourth version of the Creative Commons (n.d.) license suite. In this version, as opposed to creating derivative versions for each country, the lessons learned from that process were combined in an attempt to create a single internationally applicable set of licenses. This process was entirely dependent on the experience of the international chapters and porting process as well as the capacity to integrate and synthesize that expertise and experience.

are subject to) different settings at the same time. For example, in countries where markets are opening up, rigid control over family relations (private life, gender roles, etc.) may increase (i.e., where inequality is social rather than economic). Political and commercial discourses routinely cite fear of disorder or chaos to justify authoritarian control, but that supposed "solution" (command and control) is just as dangerous. Political disputation is properly about whether more control or openness is required in any given setting. The challenge for policy makers and leaders is to find the optimum point of poise, without knowing it in advance, and then keep the actual situation for any given instance as close to that point as possible.

Digitally mediated shifts in the underlying economics of knowledge production have given rise to new business models and institutions. Newly empowered groups working beyond the bounds of formal institutions are challenging the roles of traditional knowledge brokers, from Wikipedia to the Khan Academy offering free online education anywhere, to hyperlocal community news and affinity groups. In the face of this challenge, particularly where seen as a threat, the risk is that universities will default to being closed. Focusing on traditional networks of knowledge exchange and production is likely to reify these closed structures. In a changing and increasingly uncertain world, universities risk failure or at least a dystopian future if they follow the default path.

This model of knowledge production poised on a boundary between order and chaos implies a need for a dynamic process in which work is required to maintain complex balance. The trick for analysts is not to argue for one extreme or the other. Instead, it is to gather and sift the evidence to work toward this point of dynamic stability that maximizes flexibility and resilience, but also creativity and knowledge creation. Our role is to argue for moving technical, political, and commercial control practices nearer to that poised point, and marshal the evidence on the best route(s) forward.

2
Knowledge

Knowledge is described, exploited, analyzed, and studied in many different ways. Different scholarly disciplines think of the "stuff" of knowledge through radically different frameworks. Epistemology, sociology, and cultural studies think in distinctive ways about what knowledge is. Communities outside the formal academy, including journalists, industrialists, politicians, policy advocates, and judges as well as different publics, have different understandings of knowledge along with differing expectations of the groups that claim to produce it.

We advocate for universities as OKIs that institutionalize diversity and, working with the broader community, contribute to a common pool resource of knowledge. To imagine universities as open knowledge institutions, we need to discuss these forms of knowledge, leading to the different ways in which knowledge has been conceptualized as a good in the knowledge economy.

In this chapter, we present "knowledge" in various methodological interpretations, particularly from scientific, economic, systemic, and cultural perspectives. While these views do not necessarily coalesce, they present the potentialities and limitations of open knowledge and OKIs in several different lights.

Knowledge and Culture

Information is everywhere. On the basis of its building blocks, we may develop knowledge. Occasionally, some forms of knowledge will be accorded the status of wisdom. More often wisdom is incorporated into implicit (Collins 2010) or "craft" (Ravetz 1971) knowledge of communities. Education deals with existing knowledge and its transmission. Research institutions value new knowledge. To be worthy of a research degree, students are required to make "a genuine contribution to knowledge." The skills required to produce that contribution are highly prized in themselves as well as in their direct or indirect applications. Culture is essential in determining what knowledge means and who gets to share it (Hartley 2018). One culture's knowledge may be another's cultural noise, proving to be meaningless or meaning something quite different in other cultural contexts. Most cultures, however, distinguish formal, certified forms of knowledge—sanctioned by publishing houses, libraries, or national institutions—from informal, unsanctioned forms of knowledge, the most ubiquitous evidence of which can be found in today's social media.

Knowledge is global. This sometimes brings different knowledge systems into conflict. Different levels within a knowledge system also come into conflict, for example, when the micro (agent/text), meso (institution/discourse), and macro (system/network) levels interact (Knowledge Exchange et al. 2019). As information became capable of instantaneous global transmission with the advent of the telegraph, knowledge also took on more universal characteristics. But as the proportion of populations sharing in that knowledge has grown and accelerated in the last half century, knowledge has tended toward a distinctive bifurcation into "violent-productive" knowledge in contrast to "tribal-connective" knowledge. John Hartley (2018, 28) distinguishes "deep, specialist, expert, disciplinary and literate" productive knowledge, claimable as intellectual property, from connective knowledge, which is "broad, circulating in every-day language and popular culture, open to everyone."

While the productive, sanctioned knowledge might once, in the Western tradition, have been written in Latin, the connective type was once only orally communicated in the local vernacular. Now in the age of multimedia, all knowledge types appear across all communication forms. From the perspective of institutions of learning, a huge and unresolved question is how much, and how consistently, unsanctioned (connective) knowledge is relevant to the role of formal (productive) learning or discovery. How much should it be embraced or excluded? This question is particularly challenging for an aspiring OKI with strong foundations in local communities extending beyond the existing, carefully selected elites.

Another way of thinking about knowledge is to distinguish between know-how and know-what. Know-how is frequently less sanctioned and formal, and not a basis of knowledge in traditional universities. Know-what is seen as the basis of scientific knowledge—the building blocks of the scientific method. Indigenous knowledge

---

Case Study 5
Fake News

Over the past few years, social and mainstream media have been flooded with what a University of Münster study dubs "pandemic populism," where verifiable news is laced with ideological poison, often pursuing an alt-right political agenda (Boberg et al. 2020; DW 2020). Thus "openness" in science contends constantly with another kind of openness, where freedom of speech serves power plays rather than truth seeking. This is the terrain of "fake news," on which much has been written in news media and scholarly publications. By this time, fake news is not so much a wrong to be righted or scandal to be exposed as a meme to be deployed by all-too-knowing subjects.

What can an OKI do about it? The answer will depend on the context, but it may include play: "Break your own news: This app is intended for fun, humour and parody—be careful what you make and how it may be shared. You should avoid making things which are unlawful, defamatory or likely to cause distress. Have fun and be kind!" (https://breakyourownnews.com/).

Case Study 5 (continued)

The point has certainly been reached when fake news is itself a prime example of fake news. It's hardly worth anyone's further attention to associate it with a given actor (Donald Trump) or agency (CNN). As we write, Google's top suggestions for the search item "fake news" are "game" and "generator"—for users who want to play with the concept, not to have it explained to them. Even Google Scholar suggests "humor," "the onion," and "satire" along with "real" and "journalism." One philosopher has recommended that scholars "stop talking about fake news!" (Habgood-Coote 2019) because its meaning is contested, it's not the best term for "epistemic dysfunction," and its use is generally propagandistic.

If you can't tell what's fake from what's real by checking the identity of the author or outlet, then perhaps the problem lies not so much with the actor or agent but rather with "a more recently popular addition to the tree of binaries": the binary of "real : fake" itself. Journalism scholar Tamara Witschge and her colleagues (2018, 656) have confronted the issue, recommending that we use instead an *"experientialist"* approach that acknowledges that "we *understand* the world through our *interactions* with it," following the germinal work of George Lakoff and Mark Johnson (1980). They recommend a form of openness that admits of new values and knowledge:

> Such an answer to the increasing complexity of the social world does not rely on reductionism, but is focused on expansion. It allows us to provide inclusive accounts of this world, messiness and all. In that we may need to develop values that are now perhaps rather marginal if guiding our practices at all, such as doubt, making (and staying with the) trouble, staying present, and being open: "open to the data, open to being wrong, to redoing one's own work, actively to seek out new views and mistakes." (Witschge et al. 2018, 657)

They suggest a practical way "to address this empirical challenge of an experientialist approach is to take *situations* as the unit of analysis, rather than the social actors" (657).

People are used to working within "situations" (Potts et al. 2008), adjusting their understanding of truth and deception through their interactions with the constellation of interlocutors, purposes, and powers in which they find themselves. Social media are no different, and attempts to shame particular sources or speakers as fake can be seen for what they are: a language game.

It is true that in politics, the stakes of such games are high, but that doesn't alter the situation or genre. Contemporary literacy—both digital and social—imposes the need for widespread openness to the skills of situated interpretation. It is clear that popular culture itself is on the case, and institutional reform can learn from it.

can present fundamental challenges in terms of both methodological compatibility and the inclusion or exclusion of audience.

Knowledge as an Economic Good

Knowledge is frequently imagined as an economic good, whereby it is accorded a certain type of value. In particular, it is seen as production, whose inputs can be put to other uses and that requires coordination. The quality of the organization (i.e., the governance and infrastructure of production) and translation of these inputs into outputs are the basis of the economy of knowledge production. There are several institutions engaged in this production, though they differ in how these economic goods are conceived of—variously as private good, public good, club good, and common pool resource.

The production of knowledge is often, mistakenly, thought to be a public good. It is certainly true that new knowledge does have characteristics of a public good, in the technical economic sense of that term. That is, knowledge is expensive to hold exclusively and does not lessen in value when shared. Yet new knowledge also has characteristics of a private good, where exclusion can be created through secrecy, for instance, by simply not telling anyone, or club good, wherein members of privileged groups (e.g., medieval guilds or industry associations, or subscribers to a specific journal) are able to maintain ownership of valuable knowledge.

Notions of ownership oftentimes serve as organizational mechanisms in economies of knowledge, such as markets that are organized around intellectual property rights or the commercialization of knowledge. These are most easily observed in terms of corporate laboratories that are organized primarily around the exploitation of knowledge for financial gain. Private organizations, which operate with knowledge as a private good, are typically controlled through public regulation. Club goods, such as consortia of research organizations, also rely on governance mechanisms to control access to the "good"—that is, knowledge.

Knowledge can also be organized through the commons, in which knowledge is considered a common pool resource (Ostrom 1990). This is different from knowledge as a private or public good, thus transcending purely economic categories. In a common pool resource, a community comes together to create rules of governance (institutions) for the creation, maintenance, and use of the common pool resource based on mutually shared values and moral commitments. This works through community-created rules, not through legislation, regulation, and public fiscal funding (as in a public good), or markets and hierarchies (as in a private good). Common pool resources are usually difficult to create because governance is hard, but are frequently the most efficient institutional form for the production and consumption of goods under a wide variety of circumstances, superior to both public and private forms of governance.

Knowledge in the Public Interest

In discussing knowledge specifically, but in other cases too, there can be a confusion between the economic language in which it is referred to (incorrectly in our view) as "a public good" and the quite different point of the production of knowledge being "for the good of the public" or in the "public interest." Approaching knowledge as a common pool resource differs from the economy of knowledge in terms of the role of public interest, as embedded in a community of knowledge producers and users. The theory of social choice has shown that there is no way to aggregate individual interests consistently into one single proposition of public interest. In fact, this requirement would imply that knowing the public interest results in systemic closure. This dilemma has been succinctly analyzed by Amartya Sen (2009) in his *Idea of Justice*, where he provided the systematic reasons why the public interest can only be defined via a process of deliberation that is as inclusive as possible, and entails a process of forming and transforming individual interests via an open public discourse.

Yet as Sen also has shown, the challenge emerges as to whether we define "public" in the context of local and national societies, or establish a global reference frame. A deliberative process in a rich country might result in the institutional choice to declare the physical comfort of elderly citizens as a public interest (perhaps including certain public national health care services), while at the same time ignoring pressing public health issues in poor developing countries. This problem has been highlighted by global philanthropic initiatives to support research on malaria, for example. It suggests that a system of producing knowledge as a common pool resource must be grounded in an open public dialogue about the adequate forms of institutionalizing it within a specific domain, such as certain areas of public health, pharmaceutical research, and medicine. This requirement is, in turn, based on the idea that the system itself is in the public interest.

This assumption is a value proposition that needs to be put into the perspective that the openness of knowledge can be a private economic good as well; this is often the case in fields of technological innovation where network externalities loom large (e.g., Tesla opening access to large segments of its patents). This does not mean that less access would be in the public interest either. The more fundamental question is whether institutional forms of economization of any kind, private and public, are in the public interest, or knowledge should be produced as a common pool resource.

This question is especially virulent if we consider different forms of knowledge. Economization is frequently the default option regarding all forms of productive knowledge (the sciences, medicine, engineering, and so on). Other kinds of knowledge may not be susceptible to economization in a principled way because they relate to the formation of identities, create cultural values, or enable various ways of resolving conflicting worldviews. In terms of disciplinary institutionalization, these are the humanities in the broadest sense as well as many variants of social science. Since economization cannot apply, the adoption of a generic economic view on knowledge needs to be subject to considerations of political public interest. But even when considering productive knowledge, there are important issues of the implicit and explicit value dimensions of research (such as in medicine) or disciplinary cultures (such as economics vis-à-vis other social sciences).

In summary, the economic analysis of knowledge and knowledge systems always needs to be embedded in considerations of the public interest. That is, it needs to be organized as an open process of generating the knowledge about the public interest.

Open and Closed Knowledge Systems

As we have discussed, knowledge systems exist on a spectrum ranging from control to chaos. While this is distinct from the common usage of "open" and "closed," it is important that we discuss the characteristics of knowledge systems in terms of that common usage. "Open" and "closed" are words with moral orientations: an open mind signals enlightenment and charity, whereas a closed mind is dogmatic and obstinate; an open door points to the future, but shady dealing happens behind closed doors; an open economy drives wealth and prosperity, yet a closed economy is run by dictators.

The value of "open" is not a moral imperative but rather a property of a system that seeks to thrive in a changing, uncertain world, where not everything is known or can be known a priori about the world, and its possibilities and prospects. Open is a way of being, for an agent or any complex system, that is adapted to an environment of change

(Kauffman 1993). This vision of what it means to be open reflects the principles of thermodynamics (Prigogine and Stengers 1985), in which to be open is an evolutionary strategy, albeit a costly one.

An open and closed system can both survive in an unchanging world, but a closed system will do better because it will optimize according to efficiency. In a changing world, a closed system is fragile, whereas an open system is robust and adaptable. An open system can grow and evolve. This trade-off, between cost and dynamism, is a key distinction between open and closed systems.

The reason "open" has such positive emotional valence to the modern ear is that the essence of modernity is to live in a continually changing world. Indeed, to be modern is to attain stability and poise, to thrive, amid accelerating change and mobility. This is the world of new technologies, economic growth and globalization, cultures merging, and societies evolving. Knowledge (not just data, but meaning) is becoming increasingly networked. The technological landscapes within which knowledge is created are characterized by accelerating rates of change. This is creating challenges for all players in the system—raising questions of privacy and control as well as transparency and accountability, and supplying new opportunities for and ways of engaging with the products and building blocks of new knowledge.

Many of our responses to problems associated with increased rates of change are to attempt to close down (control) the sharing of knowledge (e.g., by such means as digital rights management software applied to digital publications), privatize and commercialize commons such as data (e.g., the 2018 Facebook and Cambridge Analytica data scandal (ur Rehman 2019), and increase the regulation and censorship of the internet (e.g., China's Great Firewall). Closure becomes the answer to changes instead of increased transparency and openness. This is a fundamentally flawed response, however. Closed systems are more fragile in a world of accelerating change. Seeking to harden them with regulatory stiffening only delays inevitable reckonings.

Institutions that might operate as either open or closed knowledge systems include government, funding organizations, disciplinary associations, journals, internet platforms, and so on. A key distinction between open and closed knowledge systems relates to the boundaries that exist between knowledge and nonknowledge. In closed knowledge systems, the borderline is rigid and boundary making is a top-down process. Disciplinary boundaries and structures are also fixed. In open knowledge systems, the border among knowledge and nonknowledge is endogenous to the interactions between all elements in the system. In closed knowledge systems, for example, Indigenous knowledge may be declared as nonknowledge because it does not fit comfortably within the established disciplinary order; in open knowledge systems, users may be involved in integrating Indigenous knowledge into the knowledge system. Further, in open knowledge systems, disciplinary borders are porous and always open to negotiation. In general, closed knowledge systems are hierarchical and operated from the top, placing an emphasis on control and governance.

Figures 2.1 and 2.2 are conceptual maps of systems that depict simple and ideal-typical structures and elements. In practice, the systems are actualized via processes of institutionalization. The university is one and presumably the most important form of institutionalization embedded in other forms, such as the journal system, disciplinary organizations, or government institutions. The systems can be realized as fractals on different levels; for instance, disciplines manifest a similar structure and can be analyzed within the same framework. In this case, it is crucial to recognize that there is potential for conflict and coordination failure; for example, the controlling instances of disciplines may stay in competition with other disciplines so that incentives for closure evolve endogenously. This, in turn, raises the question of how the relationship between

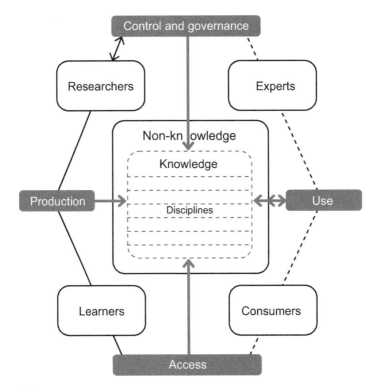

Figure 2.1
Open knowledge system.

different systems manifestations is governed. Universities may, for instance, be involved in governing the interaction among disciplines within their jurisdiction without, however, being able to determine the borders among disciplines on a global level.

One fundamental difference between closed and open knowledge systems is the role of "consumers" (users) of knowledge. Whereas in closed knowledge systems, experts also govern the use of knowledge (e.g., a doctor ordering a therapy or literary critics recommending books), in open knowledge systems, consumers become involved in the use of knowledge (e.g., patients have a say in selecting nonstandard therapies, or readers recommend good books to each other via review websites and social media). In addition, there is a feedback

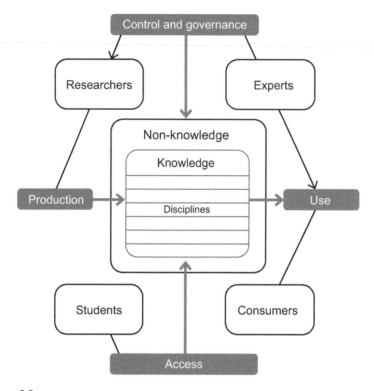

Figure 2.2
Closed knowledge system.

loop between use and knowledge. In closed knowledge systems, use may also lead to knowledge creation on the part of users, such as tacit knowledge in implementing technologies (Mokyr 2009), but in open knowledge systems, this is explicitly fed back into the production of knowledge, such as in citizen science or fan cocreation of cell phone designs in Xiaomi (Shirky 2015).

In closed knowledge systems, students have access to knowledge but are subject to hierarchical governance structures (e.g., learning is restricted to the disciplinary framework, or teaching is restricted to what is examined, not what is known). Access combines with a passive and restricted role in knowledge acquisition. In open knowledge systems, students become producers of knowledge and are active in determining the content of learning. In a similar vein, consumers gain access to knowledge (e.g., modifications of knowledge are less impeded by copyrights and patents). Other differences in access include publication practices (e.g., open access in open knowledge systems).

In closed knowledge systems, researchers are subject to control from above such as performance evaluation and limited term contracts, with research aims determined by higher-level decision makers. Often this is institutionalized in an indirect way via the organization of disciplines; peer review and journal organization, for instance, may restrict freedom in determining the choice of topics and methods since incumbents control the process (researchers who have a prominent position at the control level). In open knowledge systems, researchers enjoy much more freedom and are more directly involved in the governance process (e.g., peer review may be transparent and public, allowing for responses to reviewers).

Both open and closed systems exist in complex and dynamic networks characterized by constant interactions between internal and external actors, which all shape the ways that these systems operate and can be governed. There are more actors involved in knowledge systems, with various intermediaries such as libraries and curators, and the beneficiaries of research outputs who might not directly interact with major components in the figures, such as patients benefiting from medical research.

Under some circumstances, openness becomes problematic or even deeply negative. Common critiques of the "information deluge," prompted and supported by the openness of the internet, highlight the challenges in open knowledge. Too much open knowledge may become chaos and noise; if many knowledge objects are released in an unmediated or uncoordinated form, the results may lessen the value and impact of research and knowledge. Open may also be dangerous when it extends knowledge into places where it may cause harm, such as terrorism, exposing personal information (like medical records), or taking advantage of inequitable relationships (notably Indigenous knowledge). Even if the "good" (or commodity that is sold, traded, protected, or consumed) may offer a benefit for some, it may do harm to others. Therefore open knowledge must be embedded in systems that foster exchange and value heterogeneity to promote transparency for the public good.

Social Knowledge Production

Centrally, it is in contact between different communities creating and using knowledge that value is being created in open knowledge systems. This can be the kind of economic value captured in the consideration of knowledge as an economic good, but can also be forms of value that are not easily captured in this conceptualization, including broader ideas of "the public interest." These differences in perspective color many of the categorizations of open scholarship and knowledge creation. Benedikt Fecher and Sascha Friesike (2014), for instance, identify differing motivations in the "five schools of open science" through textual analysis of policy and advocacy documents built on concerns about economic efficiency, public interest, and the engagement of communities. Samuel Moore (2017) points out that openness in knowledge production may be better seen as a "boundary object," a shared concept that actually refers to multiple different aspects.

Finding a simple common thread here is challenging or impossible. One aspect that links concerns around open knowledge systems and concepts of knowledge itself is the idea that knowledge is social in terms of its production, capacity to support public interest, communication, and the different kinds of value that it creates. Core to the question of how universities can contribute as OKIs will be how they can support and coordinate diverse communities along with effective communication to create the diverse kinds of value (and differing values) that underlie these different conceptions of knowledge.

3
Universities

Universities as Open Knowledge Institutions

The modern research university, dating from the German technical education and research system of the nineteenth century, was built to be open to the world, pulling knowledge in and pushing knowledge out. It was a product of the liberal Enlightenment and "invisible college" (Mokyr 2017) that spanned Europe and gave us the modern conception of an "open society" of knowledge (Popper 1945).

An ideology of openness was pervasive in these early institutions. At the founding of Johns Hopkins University Press (2019) in 1878, for example, Daniel Colt Gilman, the first president of Johns Hopkins University, stated, "It is one of the noblest duties of a university to advance knowledge, and to diffuse it not merely among those who can attend daily lectures—but far and wide."

In the simplest terms, this provides the ideal of the modern research university as being dedicated to the production and dissemination of knowledge to the public. These values are echoed in mission statements and strategic plans across the world: the university envisions itself as a space in which knowledge is produced, often in collaboration with other partners, and its results should have significance for the broader community. The University of Cambridge (2020), for instance, states as a core value the relationship with society, making it clear that the university should have the widest possible access by members of the public and engage innovative partnerships with other knowledge institutions.

Several historical processes have endowed modern universities with a privileged space in the knowledge economy. Academic scholars have been ascribed certain virtues that are frequently not attached to knowledge makers in other industries (Shapin 2008). Their peculiar system of self-government, including peer review and disciplinization has oftentimes been used as a protection against outside influence. Furthermore, universities in the aggregate engage with a large proportion of the population, more than has participated in any single industry. This provides a sense of loyalty to and defense of the academy that may not be observed for other industries.

The monopoly that universities may once have enjoyed as sites of privileged access to knowledge resources is, however, being lost as digital developments make it possible for ordinary citizens to find, make, and share knowledge in open and networked systems, mediated by technology platforms and companies (Google, Facebook, YouTube, Baidu, and Tencent) rather than by experts. The growth of knowledge has been coupled with faster rates of change in all aspects of life, including accelerating technological change.

In response to these pressures as well as increased scrutiny and accountability measures, the modern university is driven to become an increasingly closed institution, which allows it to operate more efficiently to meet short-term goals set by funders, regulators, and the market. Yet this makes universities poorly suited to the realities of accelerating change and poorly positioned to engage with new opportunities. Most important, this shift means that universities are failing in their basic mission: to serve as open institutions capable of providing the knowledge and innovations needed by a world in which change and uncertainty are inescapable realities.

Closed systems are a dominant equilibrium. But to cope with change, all systems, including societies and economies, need to be open in order to benefit from experimentation. Open systems work because they are resilient as well as capable of coping with uncertainty and accelerated change. If universities are to survive and prosper, they need to shift away from operating as closed centers of knowledge production and become open knowledge institutions. In an uncertain world, systems must accept a share of "inefficiency" (variability) in order to maximize robustness. An OKI can more productively respond to technological disruption, rapid global change, and dynamic competitive pressures. Given these attributes, an OKI is not only an optimal strategy but a contemporary necessity too.

Openness is a strategy for prospering in the context of uncertainty and change, and also a principled ethical position—a humanistic liberal quality, emphasizing social inclusiveness while minimizing tendencies toward the centralization of power and unfair distribution of knowledge resources. In a world in which moral leadership and trust in institutions are in short supply, openness provides an ethical position from which universities can speak as honest brokers, interested in the power of knowledge to create positive change in the lives of the many, not the few. Openness recognizes the connection that exists between universities and the local, national, and global communities that these institutions depend on, and in turn affect. Open stances position universities as hubs within larger networks of knowledge creation, sharing, use, and growth.

Supporting and encouraging diverse strategies for sharing the knowledge being created within universities is a powerful strategy for ensuring that universities engage with changes happening beyond the institution. Feedback mechanisms, which allow universities to understand how and where they can add value to networked knowledge environments, at both global and local levels, and in both commercial and community contexts, are vital if universities are successfully to navigate the complex changes now occurring in the landscapes in which they must operate. As incumbent and emergent institutions with a great deal of public trust, universities can act as innovative partners and sometimes leaders in an open knowledge society. Adhering to open knowledge practices would allow universities to build on the infrastructure that they already have in the service of their communities of influence and the broader public.

At their core, OKIs act as networks of knowledge, spanning common disciplinary boundaries and campus barriers in order to serve as agents for societal change. These institutions operate via a set of protocols, and are governed by commonly understood rules and procedures. These rules and procedures are neither fixed nor hierarchical; they are expected to morph and change over time; they do not serve to regulate knowledge in a market-driven way. They are oriented toward the coproduction of knowledge with and for broader communities. In an open system, evaluation criteria must expand from isolated notions of excellence to metrics that include ideas of innovation, utility, and engagement under uncertainty. OKIs of higher learning foreground and prioritize the constituent communities that their students, alumni, faculty, staff, administrators, partners, and collaborators both comprise and promote.

In this environment, the concept of excellence no longer relies on particular publication brands (e.g., high-ranking journals or presses). Instead, the value of scholarship is tied to the difference it is able to make in a life, community, nation, or the world. Advancement occurs as a reward for connectedness and usefulness, not for elite recognition. Furthermore, OKIs do not operate in isolation from or competition with other institutions but rather cooperatively to create a robust common pool resource and shared infrastructure.

It is perhaps useful to distinguish the notion of an OKI from the contemporary parlance of "open universities"—namely institutions that do not impose limitations on entry (examples of which can be seen in the United Kingdom's The Open University and Open Universities Australia). Such institutions developed around principles of open access to enrollment. Most are not experimental offshoots of existing higher education establishments but rather philosophically driven newcomers created and designed to provide educational opportunities and degrees to anyone who can afford to participate. Though they share some characteristics with OKIs, particularly in their support of a diverse student population, open universities do not typically encompass the full spectrum of criteria that are imagined in the case of an OKI because they confine openness to the student demographic, and not to systemic knowledge making and sharing.

Maintaining Open Knowledge Institutions

OKIs, such as universities, create new values for the society at large through coordinating networks and platforms for knowledge-making activities, where the network itself is a common pool resource. Universities provide individuals and groups with access to a broader network as well as the reputational resources and honest broker status of the larger institution. Whereas different communities interact within the university to create their common pool resources, this interaction, in turn, needs to be coordinated and sustained to share the common good (e.g., departments compete against each other for funding and influence, which may create harmful externalities). Hence the network of interaction emerges as a higher-level common pool resource.

If we look at the history of the university system globally, the emergence of the university as a broker and governance structure is a hallmark of the US model (Marginson 2019). In comparison, power within the traditional German university has been distributed differently, with relatively weak faculty structures organized as collectives of autonomous chairs. Recent reforms, particularly the German Excellence Initiative that established Clusters and Universities of Excellence, have strengthened the role of the university as a coordinating, mediating, and enabling institution. Yet critics of the US model point to the negative, knowledge-closing impacts of a focus on rankings, the market-oriented design of programs, and the growing dependence on nontenure-track and part-time faculty (Wallis 2018). In the US model, principles of closure and openness stay in tension.

Understood in this way, open knowledge as an organizing framework is a strategy and alignment that protects the common knowledge pool resources of the university in the context of change and uncertainty. The successful management of common pool resources depends on coordination and governance mechanisms, such as

---

Case Study 6
The German Excellence Initiative

Germany's universities are supported and governed via the states that make up Germany's federal system. Traditionally there has been relatively little hierarchy within the German universities and significant autonomy for individual universities within the system. In 2006, the German government created a €4.6 billion program that aimed to help a small group of universities to challenge US and British universities for top positions in international rankings.

As with most such initiatives, the strategy has been hailed a success by its originators (Schiermeier and Van Noorden 2015). It has also generated significant controversy, however, in relation to how that success is to be judged (Krieger 2016), whether the program is sustainable, and what it has done to the character of German institutions and the German system (Brembs 2016).

It can certainly be argued that while the initiative has changed the German system and prompted greater competition among its members, not all the effects have been positive. Critics worry that the initiative has resulted in the loss of some of the German system's unique characteristics as well as the introduction of many of the less positive aspects of the British and US systems, including the casualization of staff and focus on externally provided evaluation measures. There is also a mismatch between the aspirations of the intervention and its resourcing. While the additional €148 million made available to each of the eleven institutions selected to participate in the Excellence Initiative (DFG, German Research Foundation 2020) is a substantial sum, it is insignificant in comparison to the endowments of the universities described as the inspiration for the program. Stanford and Harvard have endowments of US$27 billion and US$40 billion, respectively (Stanford University 2020; Harvard University Endowment 2020).

community norms, protocols of acceptable behavior, and a shared purpose and vision. In this sense, the university is the institutional embodiment of the public interest in creating and sustaining common knowledge pools.

OKIs nevertheless face challenges to their economic and social sustainability. The unique capability of OKIs in creating knowledge for public interests needs to be recognized and supported at policy levels, and then translated into public funding (as well as other sources) for long-term sustainability. Thus advocating for policy changes should be a permanent mission for OKIs, not a one-off distraction.

Meanwhile, as knowledge is an economic good, the knowledge object yields positive outcomes (as determined among producers and users) that are measurable or demonstrable. Open business models are therefore possible—and needed—for OKIs to increase their economic sustainability. This is not just about generating revenues from open-licensed content but also, more important, about integrating open knowledge practices with broader digital culture, economics, and innovation, thereby creating new value propositions.

As OKIs, universities must build trust and incentive-reward mechanisms for participants from academia, industry, and wider publics. This includes the development of innovative quality control methods, ranging from open peer review to altmetrics, building public trust in knowledge that is created in an open paradigm. It is also necessary to motivate both individual academics and citizens to participate in open knowledge practices and develop practical rewards for them, particularly in institutional contexts, and based on connected communities with shared interests.

Further, OKIs have both the capability and responsibility to advocate in favor of profound policy changes through analysis of good practices and evidence-based research. These policy changes include funding and evaluation issues that have been widely discussed. They will free academics from the restrictions of "publish or perish," but also avoid creating new open maxims such as "be visible or vanish."

Case Study 7
The Athena SWAN Charter

Recent twenty-first-century initiatives focus on equity, diversity, and inclusion in higher education and research to balance gender distribution among staff, especially in the STEMM disciplines, where the percentages of women are generally lower than men. In 2005, the Equality Challenge Unit in the United Kingdom established the Athena SWAN Charter with the aim of encouraging more participation by women in STEMM fields. In 2015, Athena SWAN expanded to include all disciplines, including the arts, humanities, social sciences, business and law, professional and support staff, trans staff, and students (Advance HE, n.d.).

The charter highlights the need to acknowledge and foster the talents of all persons in academic institutions, addressing issues such as the gender pay gap, short-term contracts, and discrimination based on gender and sexual preferences. Ireland adopted the Athena SWAN Charter in 2015. The Australian Academy of Science and Academy of Technological Sciences and Engineering partnered in 2015 to introduce the Athena SWAN Charter to Australia under the Science in Australia Gender Equity initiative. Currently the focus is on STEMM disciplines. Athena SWAN is an optional program, with 184 university and research institutional members in the United Kingdom, 11 institutions with awards in Ireland, and 45 member university and research organizations in Australia.

Athena SWAN has raised the profile and visibility of women among the academic community as well as awareness of gender inequality within institutions, but evidence of workplace impact and cultural change within wider staff groupings is less clear. An independent review of the UK Athena SWAN Charter in 2019 found positive effects but some concerns about superficial box ticking at an institutional level (Bhopal and Henderson 2019). An independent review commissioned by Advance HE (2020) found the charter provides effective mechanisms for addressing gender equality, yet it also identified a large administrative burden on staff in developing submissions and complying with the application requirements, and a lack of confidence in the assessment process. Both reports indicate variations in cultural change across institutions, highlighting the progress as well as challenges in addressing and achieving such change on the path to institutional openness.

Rather than building tech utopian open knowledge initiatives, though, universities are uniquely positioned to lead open transformations in a practical and sustainable way, using symbolic (branding/reputation), economic (public and/or private funding), and human (experts/ students/communities) resources. In summary, open knowledge policy innovations should endeavor to build a more diverse, inclusive, experimental, and failure-tolerant system and culture.

Opting for Openness?

Universities have many opportunities for future development. Many will build incrementally on past successes, and the development of well-tried values and priorities. For an increasing number, however, path dependence is not enough. Discontinuities or U-turns may be necessary for survival; new roles or community positionings may be essential. Many universities have, in fact, already moved toward a more open knowledge function within their communities—as "part of the world" rather than a more monastic or intramural role, "apart from the world."

Clearly a university cannot, by itself, become a successful OKI. A new institutional openness in resource availability, tying in with a greater openness in the way it runs its education or research business, depends on how a university's communities, networks, and affiliations also embrace the open knowledge opportunity—that is, how these partners seek to be involved in an OKI's new role and new knowledge emphasis. The activities of others, such as local government, religious bodies, dominant philanthropic families, and so on, can effectively usurp many of the services that an open knowledge university might seek to provide. The closed character of certain professions or disciplines, or a prevailing "key holder" approach to knowledge access, can equally thwart an institution trying to forge a new knowledge compact with its communities. On the other hand, as a trusted thought leader, a university has an obligation to foster change and confront any defensively restricted approach.

The theme of this book is that universities are well placed to take a central role as OKIs because of their liberal values, core knowledge mission, and importance in their communities. But this does not mean that all universities can or will prioritize an open knowledge role; a defense-related or religious university may have fundamental difficulties with such a role. Nor does it mean that all universities must prioritize strong community relations. Some will indeed thrive on being apart from the world, or will look for their community far from their physical location. For most comprehensive, not-for-profit universities, however, the development of an open knowledge agenda needs serious consideration. Like free trade, open knowledge is good for the system in total even when it may not always be good for any one player.

Figure 3.1 summarizes the functions that different elements of an OKI have, building on the conceptual framework developed in this chapter. The key point is that the university interacts with various and diverse external actors in creating common knowledge pools. In this interaction, the university plays the essential role of creating and sustaining a number of common pool resources that enable the actors involved. Common pool resources are created by members of the university, such as its reputation, and their sustainability builds

---

Case Study 8
Software as an Academic Output

The free and open-source software movements were significant contributors to ideas of open scholarship, and many of the disciplines with the greatest commitment to the sharing of research outputs generate software as a core activity. Nevertheless, while disciplinary communities have increasingly recognized the value of software as an output, and good software practices as good research practices, universities have been slower to adapt to the idea that software should be recognized as a product of research and scholarship on a similar level to journal articles or books.

As with the sharing and publication of data, this has led to efforts that seek to co-opt existing modes of communication and evaluation that are recognized by universities to cover software. Efforts such as BioMedCentral's Open Research Communication (Neylon 2010; Neylon et al. 2012) sought explicitly to exploit the characteristics of the journal system to make software appear valuable within journal-focused evaluation systems. In seeking to create a highly cited journal, though, the bar for entry was set too high to achieve a critical mass of submissions that met this standard. The more recent and much more successful *Journal of Open Source Software* (n.d.) takes a more "developer-friendly" approach, intended to make it as easy as possible for academic developers of software to receive a form of credit that is recognizable by their more traditional peers.

A similar motivation can be seen with efforts to encourage the citation of software. Because citations are viewed as the central metric of success for modern research, there have been attempts to co-opt this existing set of evaluation institutions to valorize the sharing of research outputs beyond text, including data as well as software. A workshop on software credit held in 2015 commenced with a session on "best practices in citation/evidence" (Software Sustainability Institute 2015), and a FORCE11 Working Group, taking inspiration from work on principles for data citation, published a similar set of principles for software citation (Smith, Katz, and Niemeyer 2016).

Criticism of this focus on citations as a means of credit has grown in parallel. This criticism comes from a theoretical perspective (Wouters 2016; Neylon 2016) as well as more fundamental concerns as to the prominence of citation as a measure for evaluation or "credit" over its original role as a means of linking related research outputs and providing the evidence underpinning claims (Bilder 2016). As one of the strongest voices arguing for the recognition of software as a scholarly output and an author of the FORCE11 software citation principles, Daniel Katz has recently explored different approaches to software citation. His reflection looked at the tension between co-opting citation approaches developed for text documents because they are coupled to existing evaluation systems and applying new systems that are more suited to software as a mode of communication (Katz 2019).

More broadly, these tensions play out across scholarly communications. If our institutions are to be open to new forms of communication, as they must be in a changing world, how can there also be coordination and agreement on what is valued? How can resources be fairly distributed among diverse activities generating a diversity of outputs, without creating incentives that will tend to reduce that diversity? How can evaluation systems be built that are appropriate to innovative forms and types of scholarly communication?

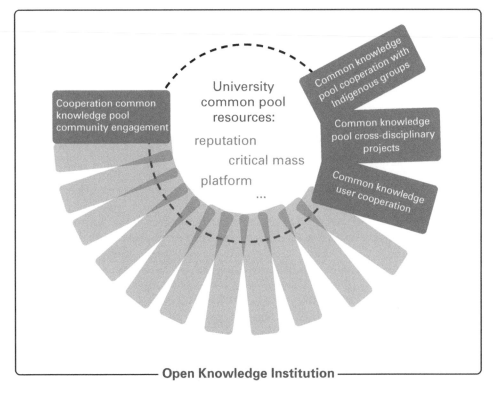

Figure 3.1
The university as an OKI.

on protocols, values, and norms that are constitutive for the university as an organization. Common knowledge pools are various but may overlap, such as including users in research cooperation with other universities as well. The entire pattern of interaction, as outlined in the figure above, is the result of the institutionalization of an open knowledge system: the OKI.

Universities as OKIs

This chapter has focused on the tensions between the aspiration of universities to be open and the default tendency toward closure for all institutions. In the following three chapters we will examine areas of activity that universities need to deliver if they are to thrive as OKIs. Drawing on the idea of knowledge production as a social activity, driven and used by communities, we frame these according to three key themes: diversity, coordination, and communication.

If knowledge is produced and used through the interaction of diverse groups, then *diversity* is a first-order principle. OKIs will need to support, interconnect, and work with communities, groups, and organizations with a diversity of experiences, knowledge, culture, and perspective. This might be viewed through the lens of the demographic diversity of the staff and students directly engaged in the work of the university, but this is only an initial step. A deep and intersectional commitment to epistemic diversity in all its forms is required.

To support the work of such diverse communities requires *coordination*. It is not productive or even ethical to simply place communities into contact. The work of finding commonalities, language, and—in the face of historical inequity and injustice—a sufficient level of trust that the benefits will be shared is crucial. In a broader sense, the core purpose of an institution is coordination. Its role is to supply common systems and platforms to reduce the costs of activity, and allow specialists to concentrate on their core skill sets and goals. The challenge in coordination is finding ways to support a diverse range of activities and actors, without restricting their flexibility. What is common is necessarily less flexible, and finding that balance is a core part of the challenge of iterating toward that point of poise between closed control and chaos.

The third critical area is *communication*. Knowledge, in all its forms, must travel beyond its point of origin if it is to support the different kinds of value creation we have described. Traditional communication of the knowledge produced in universities involves a sophisticated set of existing institutions. Some universities and some of their members are highly effective at communicating in less formally recognized ways to broader communities and publics. Supporting effective communication, writ large, is therefore a central part of what a university as an OKI needs to provide.

4
Diversity

What Is the Role of Organizational Diversity?

Our argument for OKIs places diversity of perspectives, information, and knowledge sources at the center of optimally functioning knowledge production networks. A trusted organization that adheres to OKI principles will have institutional forms that cultivate diversity through policies and actions that value as well as promote inclusion and equity across a number of dimensions. Such an organization will be able to more successfully build and participate in networks that connect diverse actors, increasing the capacity for knowledge production and the creation of value that results.

Often, conversations about diversity and equity begin and end with attention to the diverse backgrounds of individuals involved in a community, institution, or environment. This dimension of diversity is crucial, however it is also only one of a multitude of elements that contribute to an open environment for the creation, dissemination, remixing, and sustainability of knowledge, as has been demonstrated in a range of ways including by Lee Gardenswartz and colleages (2003) and Scott Page (2008).

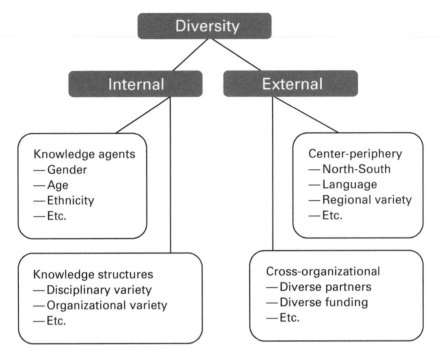

Figure 4.1
Dimensions of diversity in open knowledge universities.

Diversity is commonly reflected in a wide range of dimensions. In figure 4.1 above, these dimensions are narrowed down to a selection of aspects relevant in the university context. This includes those that go beyond the level of individual diversity. We distinguish between intraorganizational and external diversity in the relationships between the university and its environment.

- In the most general terms, internal diversity can be further differentiated into individual (knowledge agents) and intraorganizational diversity (knowledge structures).
- External diversity is manifest in the spectrum of other organizations and agents with whom the university interacts, and locational diversity in a space that is structured along the center and

periphery, such as the relative status of national languages in scientific publishing.

Diversity is crucial to the successful functioning of an OKI. This encompasses age, race, gender, sexual orientation, sexual discrimination, religion and belief, language, disability, age, ethnicity, and other categories. Openness means finding ways to support all these voices in the academy. In other words, openness embodies diversity and inclusion. This can manifest in a number of ways:

- Researchers within institutions have space for open inquiry across cultural and disciplinary boundaries, and can undertake diverse research activities within and external to the institution.
- Research within communities is community and grass roots led. The university is a partner in and not just an instigator of research.
- The form and output of research is diverse, where nontextual, visual, performative, and productive output is valued equally with traditional publications.
- Policies of equity, diversity, and inclusion in relation to staff, students, facilities, codes of conduct, and sharing of knowledge and data underpin diversity and openness in research.

Ideally, the benefits and impact of OKI equalize and include marginalized populations. The traditional disciplinary structures within universities have excluded and overlooked Indigenous knowledges (Tuhiwai Smith 2012). In Aotearoa New Zealand, efforts are being made to redress this imbalance. Māori knowledge is being incorporated, for example, into research to inform freshwater management policy and practices. Openness to combining knowledges has national benefits as well as articulating Māori perspectives and developing collaborative resource management models (Harmsworth, Awatere, and Robb 2016).

University rankings and one-dimensional quality measures do not account for nontraditional knowledge production and impacts. Worse yet, narrowly defined performance evaluations are used to quantify academic output from diverse disciplines, languages, and cultures. This means that previously disadvantaged individuals are often further disadvantaged. The need to address these issues through the open knowledge paradigm is essential.

An open culture requires constant dialogue among all the diverse actors in the institution. The value of diversity to an OKI is manifested in new internal networks and relationships among institutional actors (students, staff, alumni, core funders, and communities as well as intergenerationally). These networks enable capacity building among actors, and the creation of diverse and therefore open networks leads to benefits for the organization.

Openness means valuing a diversity of opinions, but negotiations between different claims require care and integrity. We are not proposing a post-truth era where one opinion overrides others based on power or reach, or alternately, where all positions are treated equally. Safeguards need to be in place to protect and foster differences of opinion to protect diversity and enable inclusion. At the same time, the approach to agreement or conclusion needs to be negotiated in a way that maximizes equity. Combining perspectives from the sciences, which aim rigorously to answer a well-framed question, with those from the humanities, where the questions are rigorously tested for the relations to power and tradition, will be necessary.

The risks and problems with a totally open, or rather uncontrolled, approach to knowledge production that are discussed elsewhere in this book are also particularly of concern to disadvantaged and under-represented groups. Inclusion and equity require efforts to address the risks associated with privacy/anonymity, algorithmic inequality, intellectual property, and cultural knowledge appropriation.

So how might we define the dimensions of diversity that an OKI environment should aspire to engage? The following list is not meant to be exhaustive but instead illustrative. No single university is expected to excel in all of the following; rather, it is expected to grapple with those channels that will benefit its openness. Each challenge listed below presents important opportunities to universities as emerging OKIs.

1. *Populations that have been ignored, disadvantaged, colonized, and marginalized.* OKI universities will seek to reasonably balance representation across a wide range of individual characteristics, as defined via specific sociocultural lenses. These include gender, age, ethnicity, sexual orientation, physical ability, class, religion, rank, education level, language, religion, geographic location, appearance, and other traits. An OKI benefits from attentiveness to and inclusion of a range of ages within a department.

2. *Perspectives that defy or challenge traditional disciplinary boundaries.* This involves cultivating an atmosphere in which departments do not merely replicate the same ideas or methods in their research outputs and teaching but instead encourage new perspectives and approaches. It helps to enable healthy discipline shifts and reevaluation as knowledge is created (e.g., the recent refreshing of social psychology as a discipline associated with the inclusion of researchers with a different disciplinary focus and more robust statistical analysis tools).

3. *Intellectual outputs that extend beyond the article, book, or data set.* The current academic environment credentializes and recognizes a limited, rigidly defined set of formats for promotion and tenure, degree granting, hiring, and other purposes. Broadening these to include a spectrum of outputs (e.g., digital scholarship, short-form monographs, translations, and public scholarship) empowers a broader range of voices, and encourages new forms of both research and dialogue with extended communities.

4. *Course / learning spaces / knowledge objects.* Encouraging and supporting a broader range of mechanisms for learning can enable

OKI universities to engage more learners within more creative pedagogies.

5. *Degree alternatives.* OKIs will not encourage and reward a single bachelor to doctoral track but instead may offer a range of degree forms suitable for a broader set of learners, including those that encourage partnerships between learners, teachers, and communities (e.g., certificates, badges, etc.).

6. *Collaborative partners.* OKI universities will deliberately seek to engage with a range of both internal and external groups as partners in research and learning, such as university partners from a range of prestige levels and sizes as well as nonuniversity institutions from different sectors (public, private, etc.).

7. *Cocreators of knowledge.* Universities currently focus on the production of knowledge that is then consumed by a range of players, including students, researchers, and sometimes the public. OKIs will challenge this model by acknowledging and encouraging those who engage with an intellectual object to be cocreators of knowledge based on that object.

8. *Center-periphery.* Power and status in various cultural contexts often yield binary juxtapositions and center-periphery relationships, whereby some perspectives are automatically valued more than others in particular environments (e.g., North/ South or male/female). OKIs will examine and challenge these power dynamics while seeking to include voices from across the spectrum.

9. *Languages.* The ubiquity of English as the primary language of scholarship curtails the different ways of thinking that are prompted via the diversity of languages. OKI universities will seek ways to better represent a range of languages through translations and other activities, not just to broaden readership, but to expand thought patterns in ways that increase the openness and value of scholarly thought and action.

In order to structure diversity-oriented policies as well as make internal and external accountability feasible, universities can and should develop indicators for evaluating their status as diverse organizations within the larger system of indicators used for assessing openness.

Figure 4.2 shows exemplary dimensions of diversity and potential indicators, with the dots as placeholders for a large spectrum of

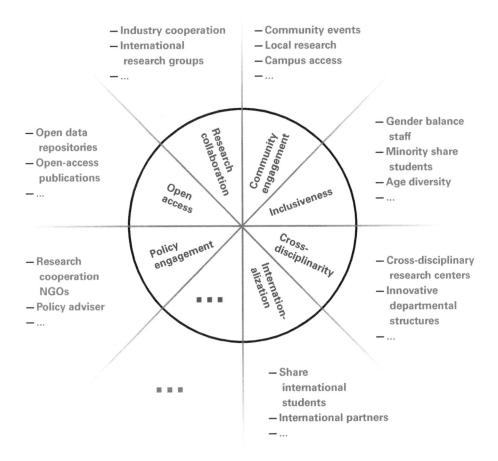

Figure 4.2
Selected indicators for measuring the diversity of universities.

other choices, depending on regional context (such as focusing on race in a South African or US context, while in Germany the organizing term would be ethnicity), demographic situation (such as aging in Japan), and other determinants. The indicators presented in this figure are arranged in open lists of categories that ensure a maximum of comparability but leave room for recognizing and expressing individual approaches and local context. The inner circle identifies categories that are universally seen as being relevant for assessing openness (such as open access) and diversity (such as inclusiveness). Within these categories, which enable comparability, universities may set up a tailored system of specific indicators (such as age diversity in the inclusiveness category).

Such a system needs to be geared toward the need for internal and external reporting. These perspectives differ because internal reporting also may be conceived of as an instrument for implementing university-wide strategies and communicating policy directions to its members, whereas external reporting may be more focused on aspects of comparability in the context of competition for researchers, students, or funding. Both are connected via the requirement in institutional evaluations to make transparent how diversity policies are designed and implemented internally.

In an OKI, however, the choice of an indicator system needs to be subject to an open and inclusive process that is not simply determined by the upper-hierarchical levels. In other words, it is essential that the construction of an indicator system is regularly reassessed in a university-wide deliberation that may include external concerned parties too. In measuring diversity, it is important that needs for including specific aspects are identified via an open discourse. This necessarily implies that an indicator system cannot be imposed by an external agency, even though these are free to construct such indicator systems in their own domain of expertise. To sum up, the diversity of OKIs is reflected in the diversity of indicators and indicator systems.

Building Trust

We have addressed the question of internal diversity within an organization such as a university. But what about diversity across organizations? How can the concept of OKIs be applied internationally? And is the OKI a mechanism through which positive change can be supported in the context of geographic inequities such as the North-South divide as well as the best and worst aspects of globalization? There are also hard questions to be asked about hierarchies of knowledge and their relationship to open knowledge. Awareness of and sensitivity to diversity in conceptions of knowledge in different cultural, political, and economic contexts is needed. So too is a commitment to ensuring that OKIs do not merely reinscribe those existing inequities.

There needs to be an understanding of how open knowledge will operate in a postglobalization era where trends toward nationalism and the closing down of free trade agreements may reduce or restrict the sharing of knowledge. What is currently happening in southern Africa, for example, is that careful and detailed consultation and dialogue between the traditional communities is building up trust and mutual understanding, creating spaces in which sensitive community knowledge is closed off and protected, while the OKI as a neutral movement can transcend some of these barriers, leading to inclusivity and openness.

The question is not only how to develop free and open knowledge sharing but also how to manage failure. It appears that the OKI as a neutral movement can transcend those barriers most effectively through careful and honest collaboration in order to lead to inclusivity and equity. Such collaboration is beginning to happen in extensive dialogue between traditional communities and trusted mediators from a range of specialist NGOs and public benefit organizations. More of these efforts are needed to ensure a democratic understanding between the parties involved in discussions.

Case Study 9
Chinese Open-Access Journals

In China, journal publishing is an area in which the state continues to play a central role. Scholarly publishing and communication infrastructure are viewed as central to China's economic ambitions, and too important to be left to the vagaries of commercial markets. State support for scholarly communication is widespread, ranging from government investment in the Chinese National Knowledge Infrastructure Network (n.d.)—a national-level database for journals, theses, conference papers, and other scholarly outputs—to subsidies paid directly to individual, frequently small-scale journal publishers. As a result, China's scholarly publishers are able to operate in a funding landscape that is relatively protected from the financial challenges of a market-based sector. For their part, Chinese libraries are not faced with the insurmountable budget pressures associated with increases in subscription prices—at least in the case of domestically published content.

The narrative of open access as a mechanism of ensuring "public access to publicly funded research," which emerged in Western criticisms of commercial journal publishing models that depend on the capacity to exclude readers who have not paid for access (Vollmer 2015), is also absent in China. Chinese-language scholarly content is readily accessible to most Chinese academics and university students. Widening access to research beyond universities is not seen as a priority for either researchers or the government. The problems facing scholarly communication in China tend to be framed as relating to quality and transparency, rather than to cost and access (Ren and Montgomery 2015). Predatory "pay-to-publish" operators along with academic fraud and corruption are seen as particularly urgent problems that need to be solved if China is to succeed in transforming its research and innovation sectors (Lin and Zhan 2014). The value proposition of Chinese open-access journals centers around notions of quality, credibility, and transparency versus public access—a key difference between China and other publishing markets.

Case Study 10
Open Access and Latin America

In South America, there are long-standing initiatives and platforms supporting particular kinds of openness within specific contexts, such as Scientific Electronic Library Online (SciELO) and the Brazilian Virtual Herbarium (BVH), which both predate and in many respects outperform their Western equivalents. The SciELO initiative began in Brazil in 1997; it has grown into a cooperative, multi-institutional approach and platform that addresses many of the scholarly communications challenges of developing countries, with an emphasis on the

Portuguese- and Spanish-speaking areas of Latin and South America, with publications in English, Portuguese, and Spanish (Packer et al. 2014).

Universal accessibility and free open access are hallmarks of this largely science-based publishing platform, which provides common methods along with a federated collection of journals, books, and preprints. The open-access environment promoted in the SciELO system not only offers free access to the outputs of scholarship; more important, it supplies scholars of all levels in Latin America with a means of producing high-quality, well-regarded publications. Similar initiatives in Western countries, including the Public Knowledge Project (Canada) and its Open Journal Systems and Open Conference Systems platforms, have provided platforms also fueled by a public mission. As if to highlight the marginalization of the Latin and South American realms in the Western publishing environment, in 2015, Jeffrey Beall (a US librarian and owner of the Beall's list of predatory journals) attacked SciELO and another Latin American database, Redalyc, within his now-infamous (and also now retired) blog, as "favelas" (slums) (Brazilian Forum of Public Health Journals Editors and Associação Brasileira de Saúde Coletiva 2015). No similar characterization of the Public Knowledge Project's Open Journal Systems' many outputs was made by Beall, raising familiar questions about the "neocolonial" perspective and prejudice that non-Western open-access publishing is so often subjected to by its Western counterparts.

The BVH provides an infrastructure for gathering and making available the digital records of plant specimens, primarily focusing on Brazil and its surrounding areas. It hosts more than 8 million records that improve the availability of specimens (via high-resolution scans and information about the location, collector, and botanical name as well as endangered status of specimens). It received 110 million data requests in October 2017 (Costa Maia et al. 2017; Neylon 2017).

The BVH is not a publishing platform but rather an open federation arena that collects data from various sources and then makes them freely available via the BVH system, maintaining ownership of the data by the original sources. The progressive nature of this system focuses on collection, long-term preservation, and access provision of the collection of data that the BVH gathers. The platform concentrates on geographic data, descriptive data, and the federation of species-based information, all intended to increase the longevity of species. The purpose of this platform has been, in part, to "promote a cultural change within the upstream herbaria driven by evidence of the increased usage that comes from a shared data access platform" (Neylon 2017, 4; Costa Maia et al. 2017). The importance of the BVH as a focused archive enables comparisons between Brazilian species and those collected in many other national contexts, including Europe, Australia, the United States, and Russia as well as more geographically bounded collections in states and regions around the world.

In addressing the role of the university, we have focused first on the benefits of diversity for the university in its role as an OKI, and then on the challenges of different geographies and cultures as well as risks for disadvantaged groups. In these cases, diversity is targeted so as to increase capacity in order to more fully represent the communities of interest and build trust with the full range of communities. But this view is quite static and passive—an effort toward just reflecting the diversity around the university. In the context of the broader agenda, an OKI does more than passively reflect its environment.

The role of an OKI is contextually to institutionalize openness, including the appropriate regulation of its limitations. If openness is a poised state between control and chaos, and one that optimizes the quality of the networks through which knowledge is being produced, then the role of an institution (as opposed to merely an organization) is to organize and support the arrangements through which choices to control and release are made. In the context of diversity, particularly where we consider underrepresented and historically disenfranchised communities, enabling those communities to exercise control is a key shift in working toward being worthy of their trust.

Indigenous knowledge provides an especially clear example of these issues. The institutions of Western knowledge production have a long history of the expropriation, if not outright theft, of knowledge and frequently its associated cultural artifacts. There is little trust from these disenfranchised communities toward Western institutions. Those scholars who do work productively with Indigenous communities emphasize the collaborative nature of their work and in particular the critical importance of ceding control over choices involving the public release of information to the community.

An OKI will offer a platform that assures participating communities of standards and controls, constraining the scholar and empowering the participant. At the same time, it will adopt the principle of subsidiarity as far as is possible, allowing those choices to be made in context. Today's compliance and regulatory frameworks often create a deep conflict of interest between the scholar in the role as a partner of a participating community and the scholar as an employee of the university. There is a balance to be found between the value in developing trust with a diverse set of partners, which might include commercial partners as well as historically disadvantaged communities, and the limitations that are to be accepted as necessary to build that trust. It is at the organizational and institutional level that trustworthiness needs to be built.

These issues are neither new nor limited to Indigenous knowledges. The management of privacy for research participants and duty of care to protect from potential harm, particularly in medical research, are examples of the same issue. The societal goal of providing accessible, transparent, and credible information on the benefits (or not) of a specific treatment must be balanced against the risks of individuals losing control over personal and potentially damaging information. That balance has been struck by placing a requirement for patient anonymity in national and system-wide regulatory frameworks, complemented increasingly today by an absolute requirement for the release of study-level aggregate data addressing the treatment of interest.

In medical research, there is significant criticism of approaches to informed consent and safeguarding. In some cases, control and protection have been insufficiently strong, leading to calls for stronger regulation and management of privacy. In others, strict interpretation has been criticized as blocking participants' access to their own medical data or preventing them from choosing to release that data in an informed way. It is interesting that approaches to both providing participants with more useful and contextual information, and enabling them to share that data, and efforts to protect Indigenous communities that choose to participate in research are taking a parallel path.

The approaches to portable consent developed by Sage Bionetworks, in which participants can choose to allow their personal data

Case Study 11
Open Access in Africa

Proponents of open development in Africa tend to argue for the benefits of openness in increasing democratic engagement and encouraging development. Yet there are cautions as a result of the appropriation of Indigenous knowledges for the purposes of commercial exploitation in the Global North—highlighting the importance of decision making at a local level about when knowledge should and perhaps should not be made open. In the context of open development in Africa, with its focus on engagement, democracy, and empowerment of communities, there is a necessary stress on creating dialogue along with opportunities for the exchange of knowledge and creativity, both locally within and among those communities, and additionally in the wider regional and global communities.

A characteristic of successful projects that involve openness and sharing with Indigenous and First Nations communities is that any decision on the dissemination of traditional knowledge is discussed with the communities concerned before any action is taken, either for collaborative and open sharing, or secrecy and protection, or even commercial exploitation. Open knowledge must also respect the rights of different knowledge systems, such as those of different Indigenous peoples who may have traditional restrictions around the access to and sharing of knowledge within groups, and externally, for example, by gender and for purposes of religious or traditional observance.

A frequently cited illustration is that of the Hoodia in the Kalahari Desert in southern Africa; the San use the plant to stave off hunger while hunting. The San people signed a benefit-sharing agreement for the exploitation of the plant for weight loss (a potentially profitable commercial opportunity) with the National Council for Scientific and Industrial Research, which in turn patented the drug and then granted an exploitation license to a commercial company (Barnett 2001). The benefits were supposed to be shared with the San people, but the agreement did not conform to the Bonn Guidelines on Access to Genetic Resources and Benefit Sharing, which aims to ensure the equitable sharing of benefits, conservation of biodiversity, and sustainability of the resources being exploited. The Hoodia stands as a classic case of the inequities in power relations that can all too easily arise in dealings between traditional communities, both by national governments and corporations.

to be shared for specified kinds of use (Wilbanks 2018), mirrors the development of community agreements between Indigenous partners and some researchers. In each case, a shared platform is being developed in which explicit choices can be made about what control is retained and what is given up. In both instances, it is the traditionally disempowered partner, the participant, who is given control.

The key to reconciling this apparent tension is to see that the role of an OKI is in building the scale and value of the trusted networks through which knowledge is created. Not all nodes on this network are the same, and a diversity of connections increases the value created. That diversity relies on trust that is built on credible governance and a belief in the good faith of actors. In turn, this depends on a shared culture that values and respects differences, and seeks to build on the value that those different perspectives bring.

Diversity, inclusion, and equity start at home. An organization must first enhance the way it internally supports diverse actors within the most tightly coupled parts of its network, staff, students, and directly affected communities. It must also ensure an appreciation of differences across organizations, geographies, cultures, and disciplinary formations. In addition, it must guide—ideally through fostering a culture of respect and interest, and where necessary through consistent regulation and direct control—the formation of new connections to ensure as far as is possible that care is taken in the building and supporting of the network so as to maximize its value for all participants.

The University as a Leader in Societal Diversity

OKIs have a broader role to play in society. Within their wider communities, universities should be taking a leadership role in demonstrating how societal diversity supports knowledge creation beyond the organization's boundaries. In some cases, students may also be forces of change to the university itself. The Rhodes Must Fall movement in South Africa is a powerful example, which quickly spiraled into a global effort to disentangle barriers to diversity with its call for the decolonization of higher education institutions. A range of high-level African and international institutions have responded to this debate, raising questions of the diversity of content and language in higher education in the developed world. These are clear signs of how universities, in their current state, are well behind the times, and measures are needed to change them. Hence a university that initiates open knowledge must be able to embrace and act on such changes.

Diversity is inherent in society, and we argue that it is a valuable characteristic of society. Inclusion and equity lead to more effective communication and knowledge production as well as freedom and successful coexistence. Although some studies have shown improvements in narrow areas, it is clear there are large gaps. Even societies that make strong claims of multiculturalism, such as Australia, appear a long way from achieving this. Senior leadership positions in Australia, as in many Western countries, show a low level of diversity. In a recent Australian Research Council granting round, there were more grants awarded to people named Dave than to women (Bogle 2017). In South Africa, with a majority Black population, it is striking that there is a strong racial imbalance in the composition of both the staff and student bodies, which after more than twenty years of postapartheid government, still do not fully reflect the national demographics. This also emerges in the profile of the research publications produced by members of the university community and in the level of support that they get for their dissemination.

One of the main causes of this failure of diversity in higher education institutions is the widespread reliance, even beyond the English-speaking world, on the impact factor as the standard measure of excellence in evaluating the status of both institutions and their researchers. This measure explicitly values the dissemination of research that is of relevance to the interests of the major

English-speaking world powers. Even in the developing world, particularly in the emerging economies, the pursuit of status through the impact factor is vigorously sought via the ever-increasing production of formal publications, especially through high-status international journals, with books playing a secondary role. This results in the undervaluing of diversity in research, often relegating development-focused research and research reported in languages other than English to a secondary status.

Outside the major powers, this focus on formal publications in the main colonial languages is more evident in emerging economies such as South Africa, a country that provides strong financial support for the publication of journal articles in listed journals and for books published by recognized scholarly publishers. In this field, the preference is for international rather than local research output in spite of the strong imperatives for the conduct of locally based and development-focused research. There are, however, research departments, centers, and institutes, many of them of high quality and internationally recognized, that engage in and self-publish research aligned with national development issues and the achievement of the sustainable development goals. But their publication output is published informally, disseminated through their websites. Increasingly, these organizations have been appointing communication and publishing advisers in order to manage and disseminate their content more professionally in the interests of wider reach as well as the potential to attract policy interest and donor funding. Initially these websites posted materials with an "all rights reserved" copyright license, while at the same time expecting content to be freely downloaded by their readers. This paradox has been largely resolved through the increased use of Creative Commons licenses, resulting in an open-access research environment for this kind of research dissemination. Language diversity has also been lacking in research practice and publication.

Universities should not only be part of the process in the drive for diversity. Taking a role as OKIs, they must act as supporters of

Case Study 12
Economics and Disciplinary Divergence

Economics is an example of a discipline with a huge impact on society via the design of policies and institutions. At the same time, there is a large diversity of approaches and theories, though organized in terms of center and periphery, both disciplinary ("mainstream" versus "heterodox") and national. Regarding the latter, one conspicuous phenomenon in economics is the national ideational dynamics in catching-up countries. In the nineteenth century, German economics increasingly criticized the intellectual dominance of British "political economy," engendering intellectual trends culminating in autonomous developments such as the so-called historical school. Although this school did not establish itself as a new paradigm, it triggered productive debates in the social sciences, with the emergence of towering figures such as Max Weber. In the wake of these debates, German economists developed the conceptual model of the "social market economy" as an institutional template for designing the German economy after the collapse of the Nazi regime. Until today, its legacy has had a tremendous impact on German policies and shaped the design of important institutions of the European Union, such as the European Central Bank.

This illustration shows how progress in economics is deeply enmeshed with societal and cultural contexts, and that diversity of theories is essential for making economics relevant for the societies in which the research takes place. Today we observe a similar development in China. The Chinese economic success defies many assumptions of standard economics, but Chinese economics converged with the international standard rapidly. This is widely seen as dominated by US economics, implying implicit references to the US institutional setting. Increasingly, leading Chinese economists such as Professor David Daokui Li question this condition and work on the development of a "Chinese economics." As in the nineteenth century, economists in the catching-up economy begin to challenge the dominant paradigm of the lead economy. Tellingly, the same was the case in late nineteenth- and early twentieth-century US economics, when this country was catching up with the leading industrial economies of the world, then including Germany.

the underpinnings of knowledge production. This means taking a role as leaders in influencing and educating their communities to embrace diversity by demonstrating how it can be done, and what value is created. This should be irrespective of discipline or traditionally perceived high-impact research. For example, Adam Haupt (2014) describes how radical hip-hop as it manifests in Cape Town townships has engaged young people in debates about diversity in postapartheid South Africa.

While diversity and inclusion are vital within a university, they should not be bounded by the university. The first step in this direction is to build, or rebuild, the trust of our communities in their universities and address the lack of trust in knowledge itself. The manifesto of open knowledge is a catalyst for taking that initial step.

5
Coordination

The Principle of Subsidiarity

OKIs model open behaviors in their mechanisms of knowledge coordination. In order to operate as effective OKIs, universities need to implement the principle of subsidiarity: that responsibility for decisions and actions resides as close as possible to the makers of knowledge.

Open knowledge systems are harder to establish, monitor, and control than closed systems, but generally bring the reward of greater efficiency and productivity. Through their commitment to forms of collegiality and diffuse accountabilities, universities are the ideal institutional base for purveying open knowledge in the broader society and act as hubs for extended community networks.

Coordination, however, also involves mechanisms of control and accountability, as required by the rules of the institution itself, laws of the land, or mandates of external regulators. The coordination of an OKI necessitates a full range of nurturing, advisory, prioritized, mandatory, and prohibitory mechanisms. The delineation of each form of coordination requires a general principle of administrative positioning in keeping with the nature and purpose of universities in the twenty-first century. Universities have traditionally been the source of expert, mandated knowledge communicated through policed pathways such as peer review. They now find themselves increasingly challenged by other forms of less authorized but no less powerful knowledge.

A principle that has often fostered the development of expert knowledge is subsidiarity. It is also particularly suitable for the development of OKIs. The University of Oxford, for instance, included subsidiarity as one of its five core values in its 2008–2013 strategic plan, believing that it should apply at all levels of the university's operations, and as both an academic and administrative principle.

Subsidiarity requires that the responsibility for decisions and actions resides as close as possible to the makers of knowledge—that is, at the lowest possible point in an administrative hierarchy. An OKI will have a high and comprehensive internal delegation of its power. If accountability could be located at the level of the faculty, department, or research center, for instance, subsidiarity suggests that the center level is most appropriate. The principle of subsidiarity thereby affords maximal empowerment to the actual producers of knowledge, but also stresses their accountability for that production and the dissemination of that knowledge, all within the prevailing rules or regulations. This is in contrast to top-down control mechanisms, which while easier to administer, strip authority from the actual producers of knowledge, thereby diminishing the rewards from yet also responsibility for their knowledge-making activities.

Because an OKI involves extensive porosity with external communities and individuals, and hence a partial responsibility for such activity, it has to have flexibility in all its negotiations with these external bodies, each of which will have their own forms of facilitation and control. These external parties include private companies, other institutions (not necessarily education or research focused, or dedicated to open knowledge), professional bodies, funding authorities, bureaucracies, and regulators. Issues of different disciplinary traditions, conflicting ethics, policy formulations, or change mechanisms as well as naked self-interest need to be encompassed in such negotiations (and subsequent documentation) of universities in developing and maintaining their open knowledge roles.

The danger in fostering open knowledge is that major breaches of agreements or regulations do occur. The 2018 Facebook–Cambridge Analytica debacle, also involving the University of Cambridge and its staff, highlights the need for careful monitoring and control, not just of knowledge and data flows, but of personnel with multiple allegiances. Institutional ethics committees must establish new regulations around individual-level data too in order to ensure that open data does not threaten the privacy of research subjects or put them at undue risk.

The solution to such problems is not, however, for universities to default to closed knowledge systems.

Knowledge Functions

Coordination in OKIs involves both internal and external partici-pants in creating, mediating, and governing knowledge. This requires navigating a complex interplay of various actors, with differing lev-els of participation and control in the system, and where the bound-ary between external and internal is increasingly and productively blurred. Functions of the knowledge production process in the uni-versity setting include:

- *Knowledge regulation*: This function is distributed throughout the organization using the principle of subsidiarity. In the OKI, protocols coordinate at the level of responsibility. *Creative Commons* is one example of scalable knowledge regulation.

- *Data sources*: Human subjects are the source of data from which knowledge is produced in the medical and social sciences. Yet the recent use of data from social media and sensor technol-ogy has vastly increased the level of personal data that are constantly recorded and used for research purposes. Research participants are increasingly unaware of their participation in research (e.g., as demonstrated by Adam Kramer, Jamie Guillory, and Jeffrey Hancock (2014) in the Facebook emotional contagion experiment). Therefore we consider those individuals who are generating data for research, with or without consent, to be participants in an open knowledge environment, requiring respect for these individuals, and consideration for their privacy and risk.

- *Spatial coordination*: The OKI has a physical as well as intellectual location. Campuses need coordination along with courses. University visitors organize their interaction with the institution (cars, coffee, infrastructure, and buildings) around campus spaces. Users of the OKI also find places in which to coordinate their own activities; an "open campus" will often present as a public park or cityscape rather than as an institution.

- *Coordination of openness*: Openness does not just happen. The OKI values standardized protocols and interoperability, ensures the findability of open data and archives, and keeps its web interface legible to those within and outside the institution. The open institution coordinates its navigability.

- *Knowledge production*: An OKI takes a social approach to the production of knowledge. This includes the contribution of identifiable social groups such as Indigenous populations, citizen scientists, and so on, but also the combined efforts of many people in the research process.

- *Knowledge mediation*: This function provides links among knowledge makers and knowledge users. As a hub for networked science and knowledge production, OKIs play a crucial role in mediating and facilitating knowledge creation and communication.

- *Knowledge curation*: In the open environment, the discoverability, accessibility, and interoperability of knowledge resources are as important as their creation. OKIs need to coordinate production, curation, exhibition, and archiving.

- *Knowledge use*: The OKI does not constrain knowledge use; it coordinates feedback, and develops protocols for the legal, ethical, and commercial use of knowledge products.

- *Social benefit*: It is always challenging to measure the benefits of knowledge for society at large. Some academic evaluation systems discourage researchers from engaging with external parties that do not directly interact with the institution or knowledge creation process, such as patients who may benefit from the outputs of medical research; lifelong learners who use open educational resources developed from research outputs, and ethnic and minority groups that have been the subject of research, among others. Such groups are a crucial part of the impact profile of institutional research. An OKI uses a participatory approach to identify problems and set research agendas in dialogue with external parties. An example would be the efforts of the Dutch government (via the Netherlands Organisation for Scientific Research) in inviting citizens to participate in the development of the national research agenda, thereby making visible the social benefits of publicly funded research.

OKIs facilitate participation rather than taking a top-down, controlling, and exclusive approach. Coordination procedures seek to enable productive and collaborative linkages with various actors, stakeholders, the grass roots, and regulators (figure 5.1).

Inclusive coordination not only provides platforms for dialogue among participants but imagines permeability among types of knowledge participants too. That is, an OKI imagines the possibility that a knowledge "consumer" can become a user, and a "beneficiary" can become a maker. All roles add value, and the possibilities for simultaneous and sequential embodiment in various roles must be maintained. Furthermore, it must be recognized that knowledge production involves many different value systems. An institution may be subject to certain regulatory frameworks that a knowledge maker may not. In turn, the knowledge maker may be responding to disciplinary pressures that are external to the institution. Coordination requires awareness of as well as attention to these competing priority and value systems.

Sensitive coordination will always maintain a precarious balance between openness and control. Actors within the knowledge system are subject to different pressures and regulation. To attend to these pressures, coordination must ensure maximum flexibility while meeting the needs of accountability bodies and regulatory agencies. Given that systems are apt to evolve to a naturally closed state, mechanisms must be in place to incentivize and reward openness.

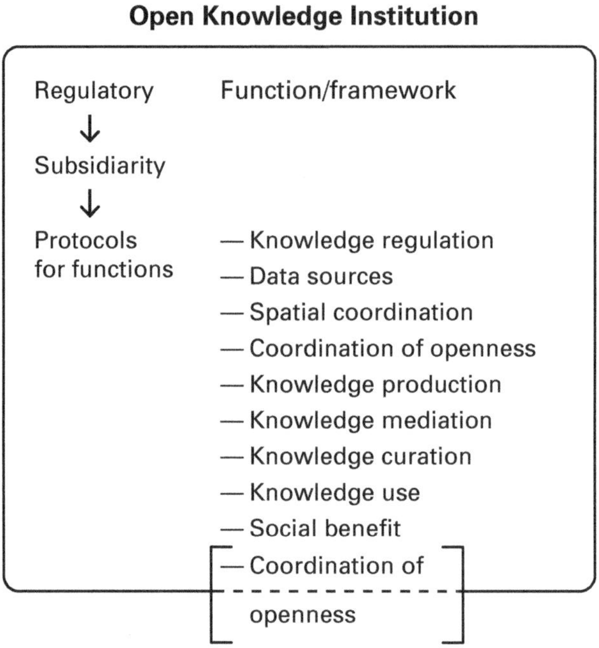

Open Knowledge Institution

Regulatory   Function/framework
    ↓
Subsidiarity
    ↓
Protocols   — Knowledge regulation
for functions   — Data sources
                     — Spatial coordination
                     — Coordination of openness
                     — Knowledge production
                     — Knowledge mediation
                     — Knowledge curation
                     — Knowledge use
                     — Social benefit
                     — Coordination of
                       openness

Figure 5.1
Coordination of functions in an OKI.

Coordination and Indicators

In 1991, Paul Ginsparg launched arXiv, the first internet-based pre-print server. It became one of the first internationally used scholarly web resources. The intention was to provide an online mechanism to facilitate the established system of preprint exchange within the field of high-energy physics. The server became well established, not only in physics, but in mathematics and computer systems, and is now the largest operating e-print system in the world. This system has replicated many traditional journal functions, such as the certification of priority claims and dissemination. The ubiquity of this platform has led to a scenario in which there is a high risk to maintaining closed dissemination (i.e., publishing exclusively in a non-open-access journal). Those who choose, for example, to publish in a non-open-access journal may be undercut by those who make their work available on arXiv. High-prestige journals have acknowledged and validated this approach, noting the benefits that accrue to scholars through openness (Larivière et al. 2014).

Despite these successes, many disciplines still encourage closed systems. Chemistry, for instance, is a notable domain with low rates of openness in scholarly communication. This disparity demonstrates the need for coordination; it is not strategically beneficial to be one open institution among several closed systems. An entire system must adapt in order for the system to regulate openness effectively and comprehensively.

If universities were to shift on a large scale to act as OKIs, this would tend to shift the equilibrium position within the overall system toward open as a default position. To depart from this norm, therefore, would come at a cost to the closed institution.

Indicators are tools commonly used to incentivize behavior in academic institutions. In a well-coordinated environment, indicators can be useful tools for developing and operationalizing norms.

Thus by developing a set of indicators of openness, it would be possible to both examine the growth of this openness and equate prestige and reputation markers with the ideals of openness.

There are, of course, certain advantages and disadvantages to being a first mover in the establishment of a new system. High-prestige institutions have the greatest potential risk, with little initial benefit. These institutions are prestigious on the basis of established systems of indicators and so have little incentive for change. Nevertheless, they also have the greatest potential to affect the system. In the establishment of open-access mandates, for instance, the adoption of policies at Harvard University (Suber 2008) and, around the same time, the US National Institutes of Health were fundamental to establishing the open-access movement as both legitimate and aspirational.

Notably, these examples involved prestige, but also exposed the negative effects of being closed. In the case of the National Institutes of Health mandate, researchers who did not comply with the requirement to deposit publications in an open-access repository would not receive funding. In this way, there is a coercive aspect to systemic coordination: one must empower individuals within the system, but there must be types of control to encourage the shift to participation in open practices too.

One of the difficulties in coordinating open knowledge practices at the institutional level is that institutions are often subordinate to disciplines in terms of authority. Institutions must be responsive to regulators, yet individuals frequently garner recognition and prestige not from their institutions but instead their disciplines. There are, of course, examples of disciplines that have been heavily supported, and thereby regulated through governmental and other institutional initiatives (such as nanoscience, neuroscience, and genetics). Yet by and large, academics are responsive to disciplinary traditions. Therefore coordination must involve engagement with these disciplinary communities. Decision makers within disciplinary communities must be engaged with and promote cultures of openness, such as editors and governing boards of professional societies. Without buy-in from these highly influential communities, the shift to open institutions at the system scale is likely to fail.

A coordination scheme should be consistent with the overall institutional tone. That is, coordination of an OKI requires that openness be embedded in the strategic plan of the institution and pervasive across all its practices. An ideology of openness cannot be mere rhetoric. Rather, an institution must be open across the range of education, research, negotiations with staff and alumni, development, and philanthropic engagements. There must be purposeful coherence in an OKI; one cannot have a closed education system in an open knowledge university. An open knowledge system requires coordination and coherence across all activities of the system.

Key Issues of Coordination

Coordination requires both a change in cultural values and the requisite infrastructure. Returning to the example of the National Institutes of Health, one can see the necessity of supporting platforms for open knowledge practices. The implementation of the National Institutes of Health's (2015) Plan for Increasing Access to Scientific Publications involved coordination with not only federally funded investigators but also the publishers to which these investigators submitted their research and the US National Library of Medicine, which maintained a repository of open-access articles. The strong coordination among these different actors, plus the financial support of infrastructure, made the National Institutes of Health's plan a success. At present, there is nearly 100 percent compliance among researchers funded by the National Institutes of Health. This is in stark contrast to the US National Science Foundation mandate, effective as of August 2013; it did not involve coordination among stakeholders nor any additional funding for infrastructures for openness. In turn, the rates at which foundation-funded researchers are making their research openly available is only slightly above those of nonfunded researchers in the United States (and compliance is at less than 50 percent) (Larivière and Sugimoto 2018). Coordination must therefore involve communication among many regulators and service providers as well as a commitment to infrastructure.

An OKI cannot exist in isolation. The infrastructure for OKIs involves coordination not only within institutions but also across them. Technical solutions for an OKI must be coherent with the principles and values of open knowledge—that is, they must facilitate maximal involvement and be inherently transparent. Blockchain technology, which is the emerging consensus protocol behind cryptocurrencies such as Bitcoin, provides an example of a technology that embodies the ideology of openness (Allen et al. 2020). Blockchain technology is, in essence, an open-source software protocol for creating and transacting value in systems without relying on centralized institutions to validate or authenticate changes to the underlying facts or entries into the ledger. Blockchain technology can be used to record and authenticate, through time-stamping and hash signatures, the exact moments of creation, and verify the originality of documents and content. This becomes a basic technology for the creation of the digital infrastructure of open systems through decentralized record keeping, auditing, verification, and cryptocurrency tokenization, thereby creating high-powered incentives for contributions to common pool knowledge and content resources.

While the primary focus of this book is on open knowledge and the university, the question of coordination goes far beyond the university campus. Given the important (although diminishing) role of government-originated funding to a university's accomplishment of its purposes in so many countries, the effective coordination of open knowledge at a systemic (macro) level hangs on effective public policy that informs funding distribution. The strengthening requirement over the last decade that recipients of public funding must provide public access to the research or educational findings resulting from such investment has been a major factor in fueling the open knowledge movement. This affects not just the various open-access initiatives in publication but also denser networking across institutional and disciplinary boundaries in educational and research developments. This requirement, however, raises crucial questions regarding the coordination of multiple actors as well as roles in such areas as intellectual property and patents.

The growth of industry linkages and public-private partnerships has raised tricky questions about the limits of exclusive rights to research, educational findings, and related materials. What is commercial in confidence, and for how long it might remain so, are important questions that do not find uniform answers across institutions, especially when private corporations are substantial funders of the research. While the conditions of receiving public funding now increasingly involve public access requirements, the situation becomes murkier when commercial partners, particularly commercializing partners, are involved. The mixed model of journal publication that currently prevails leaves the critical question of intellectual property ownership unresolved, and highlights the continuing danger of the capitalistic entrapment of institutions, scholars, or entire systems, and their (sometimes enforced) alienation from the products of their intellectual labor (as Marx [1844] might have put it).

As tech giants such as Google and Facebook have transformed into the providers of digital knowledge infrastructure, operating under a model of platform capitalism, OKIs need to develop strategies and protocols regarding content copyright and data uses while utilizing these private platforms. If OKIs are to grow and thrive, strong institutional leadership and cross-institutional coordination are needed in defense of the default position of open knowledge management. An OKI will by necessity evolve in its funding sources and financial planning, because of its greater integration into a network of associated communities, and a change away from atomized, internal cost-recovery silos to a more institutional view of the costs and benefits of open knowledge initiatives. Along with these initiatives will come new emphases in infrastructure development and partnering. A global open knowledge infrastructure is needed and being developed collaboratively by numerous like-minded open initiatives and communities.

Unlike corporate infrastructures such as Facebook, open infrastructures are built on platform cooperativism, open-source models, and knowledge commons, and technologically enable and facilitate the exchange of knowledge resources in digital forms as well as interoperable ways between different formats, mediators, and platforms. OKIs need to harness open infrastructure and take an active part in its collaborative development. The coordination of these initiatives will require academic and administrative leaders who are more negotiational in style and more multilayered in managerial focus. As the articulators of institutional tone (influencing the ratio of consonance and dissonance among partners), these leaders will require specific training. Those to whom they are accountable will need reeducation in the priorities of the less autonomous, more connected OKI.

We have largely focused on the benefits of OKIs, but we also plainly recognize that there are costs. Costs are usefully separated into the fixed costs of transition to an open state—the up-front costs of rebuilding and retooling universities—and ongoing variable costs of maintaining OKIs. Fixed costs could be considerable, not necessarily as the direct financial costs of new capital and kit, but as the costs of the disruption of standard operating procedures, protocols, and expectations. These are the up-front costs of leadership and managerial effort and attention, as much as of line items in budgets. There is therefore a role for top-down coordination from federal and state ministries of education, science, and industry to coordinate these endeavors in order to spread these costs across institutions and publicly fund the transition.

6
Communication

Communication Is Central

Universities make, disseminate, and store knowledge. In an academic setting, knowledge creation is largely measured in terms of the production of scholarly texts (e.g., books, journal articles, and conference proceedings along with certain classes of creative work). These texts are initially constructed in the university but are then refined and made public through relationships with publishers (both within and outside the university). Science communicators, critics, and popularizers, often operating outside the university community, provide a bridge between these texts and the public.

Universities are also the primary collectors of knowledge and knowledge artifacts; libraries and archives serve as the dominant resource pools for the educational and research communities of a university. Each of these functions currently operates within primarily closed systems in which there are barriers to control who can create, publish, and access knowledge. An OKI is one in which these barriers are eliminated in favor of a diversity of models for knowledge production and access. This shift is one of both technical and ideological revolution. Technical solutions diversify models of production and access, which in turn provide opportunities for broader dialogues in knowledge creation.

Publishing Open Knowledge

Communication is a key element of scholarly practices, frequently serving a critical role in building scholarly communities. Early systems of the exchange of scholarly information were often premised on explicitly bounded notions of community. The European and US-based "Republic of Letters," a seventeenth-century intellectual commentary organized through the informal exchange of letters, was the precursor to the Royal Society of London, an explicitly governed institution with rules for membership and participation, and its journal, *Philosophical Transactions of the Royal Society*. Universities were not outside the publishing system; university presses such as those at Cambridge and Oxford in the United Kingdom predate modern scientific journals.

Scientific journals evolved into closed systems, hierarchically organized through an editor or publisher, and subject to closed systems of dissemination. The twentieth century observed a dramatic shift in knowledge communication from a book-based economy to one focused around journals. This evolution and rise of corporate publishing led to an increasingly closed system. At present, scientific publishing is controlled by a corporate oligarchy, with five presses publishing the majority of scientific articles (Larivière, Haustein, and Mongeon 2015). This has resulted in high subscription prices and an expensive dependence on the services of publishers maintained through bulk subscription licenses, even for developing countries. The cost for journal subscriptions now occupies the vast majority of the budgets of university libraries. This process entrenches even further the monopoly of the journal giants.

Journal publishing intensified in tandem with rising competition in universities—from the 1960s, when academics published one monograph after achieving their first tenured position, to the 1990s, by which time academics were chasing fewer tenured positions and thereby needed to demonstrate production far ahead of finishing their doctoral degree. Metrics to evaluate knowledge production increased in tandem with this increasing speed and volume of production, both individually and in the aggregate.

Metrics serve as a form of control in a knowledge system. Despite decades of critique, the journal impact factor, originally developed as a tool to select journals for the Science Citation Index (Garfield 2006), continues to serve as a dominant metric for evaluating journals, and by extension, authors of articles and the knowledge within. By providing a numerical value to journals (and thereby a rank), this metric serves to reinforce and materialize reputational signals in the scholarly publishing market. This operates as a closed system: only journals indexed by Clarivate Analytics (a for-profit corporation) are eligible to receive this indicator. In the aggregate, these and other citation-based metrics are used to make decisions about hiring, promotion, and resource allocation in universities.

As such, journals have taken a central role in signaling expertise. Journal editors and publishers largely use peer review in defending this position, arguing that the self-governance of the process of scholarly publishing serves as a mechanism to control against abuses. Yet the concentration of the reputation market among a few key journals, and therefore key reviewers, mitigates the strength of this proposition. Despite this and other biases in peer review (Lee et al. 2013), universities still see publication in a small handful of prestigious journals that maintain their position through citation-based metrics as reliable indicators of excellence. Academics signal quality to their employer by achieving publication in high-prestige journals that have a high barrier to publication because of the sheer number of submissions, preferred disciplinary content, and peer review. Universities then signal to each other along with their funders and clients the university's quality with reference to the number of publications achieved in high-status journals. In many countries, research quality exercises exacerbate this tendency to use journal publications as proxies for quality.

Publishing is the act of making something public. The closed system of scholarly publishing currently fails to fulfill that goal, however. The current system is built on a set of closed transactions that imagine knowledge as a private good commodified through corporate publishing. Structured into this system is an implicit limitation on the role of the scholarly author and their institution, with the library as customer and the researcher as consumer. The university and its community are caught in the gap as financier. This closed system of knowledge is acknowledged to be broken.

Emerging (and a few established) practices provide examples of a successful shift from a closed to open knowledge infrastructure. Preprint repositories, such as arXiv, are notable instances of the community-based exchange of scholarly knowledge that operate with limited governance. ArXiv, originally at Los Alamos National Laboratory and now hosted by Cornell University, offers a platform for the exchange of preprints—a technological manifestation of the Republic of Letters. Nevertheless, much of what led to the success of the platform is that it merely facilitated preprint exchange that was already happening within the disciplinary community. Furthermore, this platform has not disrupted the closed system of journal publishing but instead has coexisted peacefully with it (Larivière et al. 2014). Therefore it is clear that mere technical solutions will not address the problems of closed universities. OKIs are a set of integrated open practices; there must be consistency in openness throughout the production chain.

Across the academic system, there is already substantial interest in creating better networks, although these are usually cast in quite narrow terms. Many institutions are developing and implementing policies that speak to this overall shift, sometimes in response to external pressure from government and funders, sometimes in response to community and public demands, and sometimes through internal processes. By 2019, more than eight hundred organizations across the world held such policies, as shown in figure 6.1 below. Policy, strategy, and other public position statements are not a direct sign of change occurring but rather a signal of intent as well as a proxy for organizational and institutional support of change.

Investment in publishing infrastructures is a signal of real action beyond statements of intent. For example, there has been a substantial growth in digital repository platforms by universities over the past two decades (see figure 6.2 below), in part to meet the needs of these open-access mandates. Many of these repositories are under-resourced in terms of finances, expertise, and personnel, though, and underutilized (as measured by the size and use of many of these collections). Moreover, the construction of several institutional or

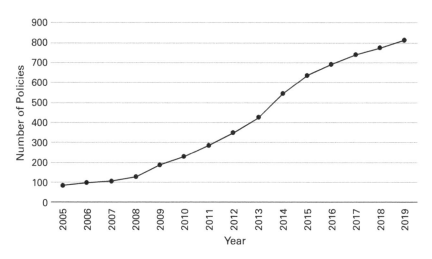

Figure 6.1
Evidence of change, with open-access policies for research institutions as an example. Data source: ROARMAP, n.d.

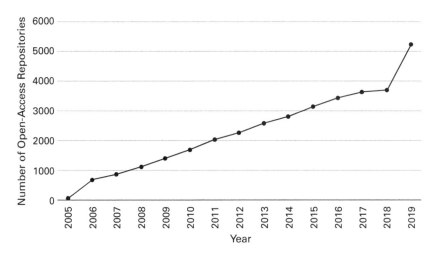

Figure 6.2
Evidence of change based on the number of university open-access repositories. Data source: JISC, n.d.

subject-based repositories does not speak to a fundamentally open infrastructure but rather one that remains bounded within institutional and disciplinary frameworks. To build OKIs across the global research enterprise, ideology must be met with a corresponding investment in shared infrastructure.

Moving beyond actions, what can we draw on as evidence of system-level change? Assessing the proportion of open access within formal traditional publications is one indicator that is becoming easier to track. Figure 6.3 below shows the significant increase in the proportion of articles published globally between 1971 and 2017 that are open access. This is also categorized into four broad routes of access. The rapid increase in open-access content provided through journals listed in the Directory of Open Access Journals (i.e., gold open access) over the last decade is particularly evidenced. Alongside this, although it is harder to track and quantify, we see increases in data sharing. Good practice in data sharing and engagement increases that visibility. All this ultimately contributes to a wider conception of publishing within institutions taking a leadership position. We also see a greater commitment from many institutions to a broader notion of publishing. Staff diversity dimensions of gender, race, ethnicity, and nationality is increasingly tracked and published, although data relating to disability appear to be a lower priority. While it is being imposed from outside the system, reporting on gender pay equity is very much on the agenda.

The data shown provide some evidence of universities engaging with open-access publication, both across the academic system and as individual organizations. There is some need, however, to be critical of the ability of the available data to inform us on progress across the full range of relevant publishing activities. For instance, the sources of data on open-access publication focus on a narrow slice of traditional and formal publications, with a bias toward publications in the English language and within scientific disciplines.

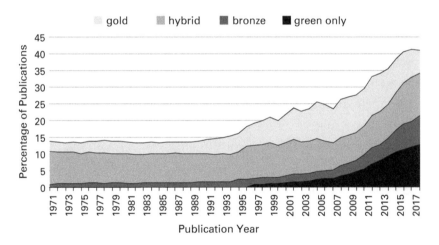

Figure 6.3
Evidence of change related to the proportion of publications with open-access copies as indicated by Unpaywall, grouped by Crossref publication dates from 1971 to 2017. Notes: Gold = published in a journal indexed by the Directory of Open Access Journals; hybrid = free to read under an open license in a toll-access journal; bronze = free to read on a publisher page without a clearly identifiable license; green only = toll access on a publisher page, but there is a free copy in an open-access repository. Data source: Figure generated using data collected by the Curtin Open Knowledge Initiative data infrastructure.

In assessing progress toward communication that supports OKIs, we must be sure not to measure only a closed and traditional portion of what counts as publication.

Mediating Open Knowledge

Digital and networked technologies disrupt the established scholarly publishing models and traditional modes of knowledge communication. They open up access to knowledge by empowering and enabling users to participate in the creation, dissemination, and evaluation of knowledge.

In a conventional scholarly publication environment, there is a narrow range of mediators: scholarly book and journal authors and publishers focused on communicating research to other scholars as well as a highly literate and relatively small lay audience; academic textbook publishers and higher education teachers; and a relatively small population of academic popularizers who are able to translate research findings for transmission through the popular media.

In open knowledge environments, though, publication is no longer simply a matter of downstreaming research in print form for distribution to the different constituencies of a traditional readership close to the academy. Open-access and digital distribution have expanded the range and reach of research dissemination. Networked technologies, especially social media, connect authors, readers, beneficiaries, and other actors in knowledge networks more broadly and effectively than ever before. Social networks enable and demand more targeted and managed mediation for much wider potential audiences as knowledge cocreators. Thereby they unlock the potential of population-wide creativity and participation in research, learning, and knowledge practices.

As the terrain of research communication has expanded, different specialisms have emerged to concentrate on the specific parts of the value chain: the production of the knowledge itself; the production of the texts arising from that knowledge; and most particularly, the mediation of the research to reach a much more widely distributed audience.

While the popularization of scholarship was a feature of the traditional environment, the scope was narrower, engaging an audience on the boundaries of scholarly disciplines. By comparison, as a mediating space, online academic news outlets such as *The Conversation* have been able to provide a translational space, widening the potential users of scholarship to target, for example, journalists, who in turn have been able to widen the readership to include policy makers, thus indirectly enabling and assisting the impact of research.

In print publishing, publishers were at the center of the knowledge production process and handled the mediation, mostly as gatekeepers. There was little need for scholarly authors to engage with the mediation of the text, other than the requirements of text preparation. This is still true for specialist scholarly monographs.

In digital publishing, mediation is primary, and mediation is nonlinear and distributed. The linear or factory model, inherited from physical communication in the print and industrial era, modeled knowledge production as a value chain. At its simplest, active agency or causation ran from the "upstream" producer (including author/artist, entrepreneur, and industrial process) through the "mainstream" distributor (transmission, including marketing) to the "downstream" consumer (passive demand or active feedback). In such a model, "open" knowledge applies to producers; consumers play little part in the process.

In a nonlinear systems environment, such as that of the digital-network era, causation is not unidirectional and linear, however, and what counts as a cause seems to multiply endlessly. We have become used to the idea that "everyone" is an author-journalist-publisher (each expression on social media can be held accountable in law as a publication), allowing for the expansion of agency, and hence creativity, across the users of a network or system. In principle, in a systems model, "everyone is a knowledge maker" within the terms of that system, making the concept of "consumer" redundant as consumers are also producers and vice versa. Hence the new importance of the concept of user.

In the digital (computational and globally networked) environment, what drives the system is mediation. In the context of what used to be called the mass media, power and profit have shifted downstream from producers (now satellite companies that supply content to networks) to distributors such as broadcasters, and more recently to platforms that aggregate traffic rather than publish content, allowing for "consumer-" and "enterprise-created content" to coexist in the same knowledge-making environment.

In figure 6.4, derived from Baran's originating model of the internet, the distinction between closed (centralized) and open (distributed) systems is clear: the centralized version has just one center of command and control while in the distributed network control is reticulated. An intermediate, decentralized version shows the "small world" model, where local organization can thrive, but the whole system remains tightly networked while internode links are weaker than in the distributed model.

In such a model, "open" knowledge applies to users. The users are part of a layered (micro-meso-macro) system of complex systems, in which mediation within and across systems is key not only to the distribution but also the expansion of knowledge.

This model of knowledge production, as the mediation of a multiplicity or plurality of voices, follows the logic of an "open" system being more robust and resilient (adaptable) than a closed system, and technological acceleration, in which the growth of knowledge increases exponentially once it is "open" to users as well as existing "black box" producers. Such a system allows for distributed expertise, crowdsourced problem solving, and innovation from anywhere in the system (such as neglected groups or regions).

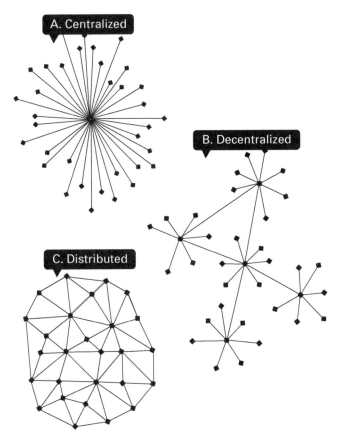

Figure 6.4
Paul Baran's (n.d.) model of a distributed network, RAND Corporation, 1964: multiple users as network nodes.

Expertise escapes command-and-control restrictions (e.g., academic/professional certification).

The shift from producer- to user-led knowledge, via mass media of communication rather than restricted institutions of learning (universities, disciplines, and specialist publishers), puts knowledge making into the same environment as popular culture, commercial entertainment, games, playfulness, and purposeless literacy, and thus places knowledge making into the same context as culture, communities, group making, identity formation, daydreaming, mischief, fantasy, and intergroup or communal conflict.

Experts and scientists who venture into this terrain used to be labeled as "popularizers" (less prestigious than "original" or "quality" researchers and scholars; this side of their work earned less institutional credit but was often celebrated when they got it right). Some like Alfred Einstein or Stephen Hawking could remain credible thinkers as well as powerful popularizers; some like Brian Cox or Neil Degrasse Tyson could build a bridge between popular and professional science, and others like David Attenborough or Tony Robinson "opened" the realm of knowledge starting from the broadcasting or entertainment perspective, with a clear feedback impact on science practice in each case. As evident from these examples, however, it is worth noting that popular science has struggled with the same gender disparities as the wider science communication landscape (Sugimoto et al. 2017).

Open knowledge is a part of this system that exerts external pressure on provider organizations from the industrial era. Thus, for instance, the hyperspecialization of knowledge into disciplines cannot survive into the open media space; here, celebrity is a more decisive signaler of quality than deep specialism, which tends to be illegible in that context. For example, in 2016, Kevin Kelly's (2015) book *The Inevitable* was published in Chinese first and promoted by social media celebrity Mr. Luo; twenty thousand copies were sold within the first two hours.

The mediation of knowledge, in addition to creation, is a key function of OKIs that connect knowledge creators and broad communities. Social media and open publishing provide both technological and socioeconomic affordances for OKIs to connect knowledge (text), authors (creators), and audiences (consumers or prosumers) in the dynamic, participatory, and collaborative process of knowledge creation and communication. This process increases the impact of institutions while driving and diversifying knowledge growth. OKIs must actively engage in mediation, exploiting existing technologies

Case Study 13
Action Dialogues in South Africa

In September 2012, more than five hundred people—including NGO activists, academics, government ministers, and policy makers—gathered at the University of Cape Town for a five-day conference, Strategies to Overcome Poverty and Inequality. The main mover behind this conference was Professor Francis Wilson, who had founded the South African Labour and Development Research Unit at the University of Cape Town some thirty years before, kicking off a long period of data gathering and research on the grueling problems of poverty and inequality in apartheid and postapartheid South Africa. Believing that solid data are the essential underpinning of good research of this kind, Wilson had decided in this earlier 1980s' initiative to publish the data online with the World Bank, yielding an award-winning data portal, Data First.

Having cataloged the data and analyzed the environment for so long, the conference was aiming, in a now-democratic South Africa, to try to create policy and practice-based solutions that would address these intractable problems. The conference provided a platform for discussion and debate among a multiplicity of participants: academic researchers, government officials, and practitioners, with a strong focus on effective, practical strategies to deal with inequality and poverty, and inspire change at the local, regional, and national levels. It gathered some four hundred papers from the wide range of participants, and these documents then needed to be published and circulated, and finally turned into a book.

These publication outputs were what would normally be expected as the culmination of a project such as this. But as Wilson describes it, he read the book, closed it, and failed to see it as closure. He began to search for an alternative kind of research output that would better utilize the interactive potential of a digital environment. What emerged was a series of workshops, called Action Dialogues, and related reports that give a nuanced, critical analysis of the current as well as possible policy interventions to overcome poverty and inequality in contemporary South Africa.

As the Mandela Initiative and the Nelson Mandela Foundation (2017) website describes them,

> Action dialogues are gatherings of around 20–25 experts from diverse sectors, including universities, government, civil society and elsewhere who meet for 2–5 days on a particular theme. The interaction that develops from these gatherings affords all participants the time to speak about their work, and discussions can begin on further possible action including how to multiply and expand successful projects. Action Dialogues are university-led but do not focus solely on academic research; they seek rather to include many of those with experience and knowledge in the theme being discussed. Thus the purpose of an Action Dialogue is to feed academic research and other knowledge into strategies and productive projects which can have an impact on poverty and inequality.

Case Study 13 (continued)

Research units—like the Institute for Poverty, Land and Agrarian Studies at the University of the Western Cape and Centre for Cities in Africa at the University of Cape Town—act collaboratively in these action dialogues, and the results are disseminated in reports and social media. These dialogues have been extensively picked up by the media—newspaper and television—and there is evidence of take-up by policy makers. As Professor Murray Leibbrandt, the current head of the South African Labour and Development Research Unit, explained,

> This is our country and our duty as researchers is to ensure that we have the right evidence in place to underpin an inclusive development strategy. We are determined to make an aggregate contribution—that's greater than the sum of our parts—to cracking our inequalities. Everyone has a part to play, from the school governing body to the NGOs and civil society organisations. We need all hands on deck. When one is in the trenches each day as part of this research unit doing this important work, you know you are doing your research as well as you can to be part of something bigger. (Swingler 2018)

---

and creating new ones that enable greater participation in knowledge production.

Collecting Open Knowledge

One of the special functions of traditional universities is the collection, reformatting, preservation, and archiving of crucial community resources. These resources may vary from the key foundational documents of a community, through vast accumulations of periodicals or newspapers, to museum collections of musical instruments, furniture, or even barbed wire. Some of these, such as original print publications, digitize well and can, with suitable licensing, be made available as open resources; others fiercely resist digitization and limit openness. To these collections, mostly of physical objects and often held in trust rather than owned by the university, a key holder or gatekeeper role is frequently assumed. Aspiring users need to establish their credentials for use, hours of visitation need to be predetermined, and a users' fee may be charged, even for members of the university itself. The digital archiving of websites, social media posts, and user-generated content all raise new issues for collecting open knowledge resources for public interests, which are increasingly valuable for research, cultural heritage, and public record. Currently, many of these digital content resources are being mediated and thus archived by commercial sectors, particularly corporate platforms like Google Books and Facebook. There is also a need to keep social media posts deleted by censors.

For decades, however, groups of regional universities have taken to the effective pooling of resources by dividing up collecting concentrations (driven by different research or educational focuses of individual institutions), facilitating interinstitutional loan and access arrangements, consortial purchasing agreements, and collaborative governance arrangements (often part of broader institutional or regional alliances). An early model in the United States was the Committee on Institutional Cooperation consortium, formed in 1958, and now part of the Big Ten Academic Alliance. By the 1980s, the committee had become an exemplar of consortial support for collaborative academic initiatives, influencing many similar developments in Europe, Asia, and Australasia, such as the "national site-license" initiative in 2001 for e-journals in Australia. Similarly, the China Academic Library and Information System, led by the Chinese Ministry of Education, is a nationwide academic library consortium for resource sharing; it integrates library resources and services, and provides digital library services for both higher education and schools.

Libraries, archives, galleries, museums, and publishers likewise have long pooled resources, infrastructure, and expertise to create diverse networks dedicated to such activities as collections management, digital publishing, and digital preservation. The MetaArchive Cooperative, founded in 2004, bridges academic and public libraries, archives, and museums across three continents into a digital preservation network that is owned and governed by its members. Institutions involved in this network host the technical infrastructure and use it to preserve their content. The web portal Europeana provides an open platform for cultural heritage materials for libraries, archives, museums, and galleries, which use it to showcase and federate their digital collections as well as address shared problems like orphaned works; similar platforms are now available in the United States (Digital Public Library of America) and Australia (Trove). In national and consortial models, these open platforms offer bridges between individual collecting institutions, and between these institutions and a broad user base that includes higher education, primary and secondary education, and public researchers.

An OKI clearly goes beyond the meso level of institutional collaboration so admirably achieved by some early consortia. This is because an open knowledge agenda involves more intensive external collaborations, both at the micro level of community individuals and groups, and the macro level of collaborations with industry, professions, and governments. Significant challenges emerge from this greater external collaboration, many driven by the unauthorized status of external collaborators within university permission systems, which is only magnified by the traditional gatekeeper role of universities over their collections, and in particular nondigital or restricted materials within their charge.

Some hurdles for the emerging OKI to overcome might include securing more community-focused licenses over digital materials, developing more open protocols for access to materials, and rethinking hours of access, user support, and catalog presentation to facilitate a more diverse population of users as well as new levels of collaboration with nonuniversity libraries, archives, or repositories.

Universities have traditionally played a broader role than simply mediating knowledge. They are institutions of civic purpose, whose own staff and graduates need qualifications for work, but also civic and cultural agents that can contribute to the construction of social

Case Study 14
Open and Library Access

Access to knowledge and engagement with external communities by institutions are important dimensions of openness. Academic libraries play a key role in facilitating and promoting institutional research and knowledge openness, contributing to and often driving open-access policy development, establishing and maintaining institutional repositories, and coordinating the deposit of open-access research output. This aligns with the underlying principles of commitment to intellectual freedom and access to information embraced by the library and information profession (IFLA 2015). Openness, though, is not embedded throughout all academic library workflows and practices. For example, book acquisition processes frequently still focus on "closed content" (Ball and Stone 2019). Further, competing demands for access to academic library physical spaces, facilities, and collections have led to exclusive policies and practices that may be seen to conflict with open-access publication positions.

Research accessible through open-access scholarly institutional and disciplinary repositories globally represents only a small proportion of the output held physically in academic libraries (for example, books, archives, manuscripts, and print journals). Constraints on unaffiliated access to academic libraries through membership, fee charging, and visitor policies restricts the usage of non-open-access current and older material in which research interest persists. A large amount of legacy, pre-open-access research output held in academic libraries may be restricted through multilayered library access policies. Fee charging for physical access to libraries and borrowing privileges applied to unaffiliated users suggests economic barriers to knowledge. This is in contrast to funded institutional open-access publishing, and the open-access movement's principles of removing barriers (Chan et al. 2002). The impacts on academic library budgets and usage from electronic resources subscriptions have driven a wedge into the accessibility to knowledge.

The open-access movement and individual universities challenge publisher controls over who can read published research. Yet library access policies do not necessarily correlate with institutional positions on open access to research publishing, expressed through policies, institutional repositories, and the extent of open-access scholarly publications. In the context of the process of institutional progress toward openness through cultural change, full open access to research knowledge continues to be a challenge (Wilson et al. 2019).

goods. A particular educational challenge lies in the retraining of specialist staff for more regular interface with broader communities along with the wider world of working with companies, multinational entities, media, and unaffiliated scholars. Universities need to develop these capabilities to educate a new generation of global citizens who can work with OKIs to forward such aims.

Rebundling Open Knowledge

The modern university is being disrupted and managerially refocused by new challenges in publishing, mediating, and collecting. The signaling agenda comes from within, as internal labor markets are considerably shaped by quality signals of individual research performance, and from without, as universities position themselves in league tables and rankings to determine their relative attractiveness to students and government funding agencies. The mediation agenda comes from their role in curating and disseminating information and knowledge—a competition in which they are ever pitted against far more powerful and agile players in the new digital media spaces. Universities are, in important ways, being strategically rerouted by these forces of mediation and signaling at large.

But some problems caused by new technologies can be fixed with even newer technologies. The first generation of the internet gave us search engines, file sharing, and social media. These also devalued many of the storage, mediation, and curation of knowledge functions played by universities, though. Many of these functions have the potential to be rebuilt within the second generation of the internet. Blockchain and other distributed ledger technologies are already being applied in reimagining how a university might function. Woolf University (n.d.) is the world's "first" blockchain university. Blockchain technologies can also be used to rebuild institutions for the decentralized storage of data and content (e.g.,

InterPlanetary File System, Storj, etc.) as well as tracking contributions and incentivizing community quality assurance tasks such as refereeing (Extance 2017).

The university has traditionally been more than an aggregation of specialized knowledge held in courses and departments. It is also a curated bundle of such knowledge—an assemblage of different kinds of knowledge that enables new discoveries to be made and new perspectives to be seen. This role is not easily played by the digital platforms of content aggregation and dissemination. So we need to re-create the forward-looking and imaginative institutions of bundling and combining knowledge in interesting as well as hopeful ways to reveal unforeseen possibilities.

7
Policy

Policy and Governance Mechanisms

Policy makers are participants in the process of creating OKIs. They contribute through the creation of formal policies and appropriate governance mechanisms. These can be particularly important, given the OKI's emphasis on coordination, which is required by the principles of subsidiarity and local contexts of knowledge activity.

Policy and governance mechanisms are systems that guide relational structures between actors within a collective body. These are crucial for the processes of interactions and decision making that lead to outcomes of collective problems. At the same time, policy involves control. If open knowledge is a continuous balancing and rebalancing between chaos and control, it implies ever-fluctuating levels. We need a sufficient consistency within this flux of inconsistency to build trusted networks among the diverse actors engaging with the OKI, whether internal or external to the institution.

At the same time, consistency is also needed for evaluation and accountability. An OKI initiates, revises, and refreshes policies, and these need to be flexible, inclusive, and transparent. These policies will enhance the ability to form new relationships within higher education as well as with external communities and users of knowledge. Openness needs a dynamic system of policy and governance.

Policy Design

OKIs apply principles and employ practical measures to design effective policies. The tension between the consistency necessary for coordination and local and contextual diversity is crucial.

In a growing number of open areas, policy design has progressed from advocacy to mandates. Nevertheless, it is important to emphasize diversity in complex policy contexts. There has been a substantial rise in the proportion of formally published scholarly literature that is free to read and increasingly freely available for reuse. This rise can be directly linked to policy initiatives, especially open-access mandates from funders, national governments, and regional coordination efforts such as the European Commission. Without some level of compulsion, this rise in accessible content would probably not have occurred.

At the same time, the focus of policy and documents from the Budapest Open Access Initiative through to funder, institutional, and national policy initiatives has left substantial gaps. The uses of mandates and the one-size-fits-all open policies are not free of controversies as they neglect the diversity of research contexts, including the privacy of patients in medical research, and disciplinary differences in sharing scholarship and research data. By comparison, policies built on the idea of being "as open as possible and only closed when necessary" could successfully address a wide range of situations.

In order to maintain diversity and address difference, we need to allow for conflict and disagreement, and understand the value of "staged" or institutionally governed forms of conflict that safeguard participants. We do not want the straw version of "safe spaces" raised by conservative critics, nor the extremes in which a right to speech has priority over the consideration of harm for others. Rather, we need trusted spaces in which different perspectives can be brought to bear. This implies an environment where modes of conflict are sufficiently circumscribed to ensure the safety of and benefits to participants. This also will protect the diversity of onward connections to the broader network that participants bring. What underpins these diverse trusted spaces is an infrastructure, "the network," both in abstract form and as an actual digital communications network with defined protocols and systems, supported by innovative policy designs.

The design of diversity policies in OKIs should also consider the various types of scholarly content and their users. Many critics have noted that merely formal scholarly literature free to read does not make it comprehensible to all the potential users of that research, from patients to businesses to concerned communities. The focus on journal articles, and specifically the subset of articles indexed in Western anglophone bibliographic systems, has additionally marginalized the influence and use of parallel literatures, including working and policy papers, that are often dismissed as gray literature.

Access and intellectual property have occupied a central place in policy design for open knowledge. OKIs will also need to design effective policies to address practical issues including infrastructure, capacity building, and community engagement. The programmatic measures and detailed policy designs may vary widely, but there are some essential and common principles that OKIs could follow.

Policy Principles

How then do we manage this tension? We need consistency and coherence, but also flexibility and contextualization. We need to support many different paths for today's universities to become fully fledged OKIs, recognizing that each university will need to adjust to its internal differences and diversities. We need to ask what policy and guidance must be shared at the global, regional, national, and institutional levels? What values and norms might conceivably be universal, and how can guidance as to their implementation best be shared?

In large part, this is answered by the principles that we have articulated thus far and further distill below. The principle of subsidiarity, for example, places control as close to individual actions as is appropriate. The extent to which that control needs to be moved "up" the system is determined by balancing the tensions between complete freedom (and potential inconsistency) and overzealous control (and homogeneity). The level of coordination is determined by the existing strength of connections in the local network. It depends on the trust between participants, current or future, and the concerns they have and risks they take in engaging. Where there is greater trust and a stronger shared culture, policy and governance can move closer to guidance and value statements. Where the network is fragile or the potential for harm is greatest, such as where Indigenous communities or patient groups are involved, greater regulation and control is required.

The logic of group governance is always fraught, and this is where policy becomes a useful tool. Ideally, the shared values of those engaged in a particular knowledge-producing group would lead them to see these challenges and incentive problems, and they would agree to bind themselves through mutually constraining yet voluntarily entered rules of governance. Mancur Olson (1965) notes that while sufficiently large groups with differing interests will struggle to agree on individual actions, particularly those involving collective goods (which include club goods and common pool resources), such groups can successfully agree to bind themselves to regulations that impose the requirements for generating those collective goods, even when it is not in their individual interests.

There will be occasions when compulsion through explicit or de facto policy is necessary too. Resource limitations may require choices about platforms that are to be shared across organizations and communities. Consensus will not always be feasible. What policy and governance can provide is the guarantee of stability. Requirements, where necessary, must take note of our understanding of the challenges of collective action and recognize that the value being created is a local collective good—one that cannot be provided by the state (here, the institution or scholarly academic system) or market—so that efforts to coordinate across groups making their own choices is crucial.

With this as background, we can articulate some principles of governance and policy that are consistent with the overall vision of OKIs:

- *Diversity* is a first-order principle, as it compels OKIs to institutionalize creativity in ways that reflect more than only local-level creations. Diversity requires ongoing work and support in the same way that openness does.

- *Subsidiarity* is critical, and the default position should be to enable action. Decisions to impose control must be driven by a clearly articulated need for coordination, consistency, or trust building with the target of a more diverse network.

- *Coordination* should be delivered through the provision of platforms where feasible. Platforms provide infrastructure at the lowest possible level that encourages the desired effect. Compliance with the platform should never be compulsory. Platforms act as guides; they do not dictate practice.

- *Policy and direction*, where necessary, should be directed at creating shared culture and values rather than compliance. The goal is observation of the spirit, not compliance with the letter of the law, even if direction and compliance are required as part of that shift.

- *Consistency* should be provided through the university acting as a platform that supports community and network building, and supplies (and interacts with other OKIs to resource) infrastructures that guide consistency.

- *Governance* arrangements are consistent with all these principles.

These principles may seem straightforward, but they imply a truly radical shift in our thinking around university leadership and strategy. They point to the role of leadership not as executives determining and resourcing strategy but instead as community builders and facilitators. Rather than acting as visionaries that stand alone, such leadership will be embedded within the community. Leaders will engage in narrative building in support of shared culture and diversity, telling the story of the organization with an emphasis on its role and connections in society.

This reformation of leaders as community mediators reflects our understanding of the successful governance of common pool resources and club goods (Hess and Ostrom 2006). Successful governance of such resources is almost invariably bottom up. Top-down imposition should be the exception. It should always be focused on coordination and mediation undertaken in the service of building and sustaining trust in networks, in addition to legal and regulatory compliance. Any such imposition must be applied at the correct level and should build in the flexibility to change over time. For openness to offer resilience, it must be flexible. Therefore the ways in which we constrain ourselves must include mechanisms for change that can be enacted fluidly when changes occur in our political, economic, social, or technical environments.

Policy in Context

Defining the ideal policy and governance approaches for a university as an OKI needs to be sensitive to context. There are many aspects of the environment of a university that are outside its control. Open institutions are especially connective as well as networked and embedded in their communities at various levels. Knowledge within these communities may be regulated by intellectual property limitations, local issues, and ethical concerns.

Policy levers at the national level can support shifts toward openness. Many countries already have open government data policies. Internationally, the Open Data Charter (n.d.) sets out six general principles of openness for data. Yet simply opening up data has not necessarily led to substantial changes at the institutional level. Continued interaction between institutions, at the international, national, and regional levels, will be necessary to facilitate the greater openness of knowledge.

Differences in culture and other contextual issues, including politics, resourcing, and local priorities for knowledge production, can all play an important role in enhancing the openness of knowledge. The successful OKI provides for independence and innovation, and does not unnecessarily close options for new connections and activities. To thrive, it will need to align itself closely with local communities and contexts, including policy makers and political leadership. The successful university will, however, through its connective scholarship, already be influencing policy making at the national and regional levels, both directly and through coalitions with other like-minded organizations.

8
Indicators

Can We Evaluate Openness?

Openness requires transparency. This principle applies both internally and externally. The members of an open knowledge institution need to know about the status of their organization, and their relationships with other institutions, groups, and individuals. They also need to be able to assess their own progress toward the goals that the institution has established via an open process of consultation and deliberation. This creates internal imperatives of accountability of the organization vis-à-vis its members. At the same time, as a public interest institution, an OKI is externally accountable toward its relevant communities and society. Both forms of accountability require organizational procedures and protocols for assessing the status of the open knowledge institutions by means of indicators.

Establishing such protocols, though, always involves a trade-off between the possible accuracy and quantifiability of certain indicators and their effects on perceptions and resulting behavior. As has been well theorized and empirically demonstrated (Holmström 2017), closed quantitative indicator systems necessarily result in two issues that are especially detrimental in the context of openness: indicators lead toward the relative neglect of all activities that are not measured by the indicator, and agents will try to game the system. If both effects come together, serious organizational pathologies occur.

As a consequence, an effective system of indicators for OKIs must combine internal progress evaluation with qualitative indicators for external communication and reporting. This remains open in the sense that it leaves room for contextualized adaptations to the environment and nature of the respective open knowledge institutions. Furthermore, it is imperative that the indicators be matched to the concepts that the institution hopes to incentivize, and in keeping with an open ideology.

Challenges in Evaluation

Within the broader scope of open knowledge along with the institutions that support and sustain it, a wide range of qualities and practices can contribute to a shift for a university toward becoming an OKI. Many of these activities and qualities already exist in some institutions and places, although with inconsistent implementation and without coherence across activities. In the specific case of universities and colleges, these activities and qualities are often not directly supported by the organization as a whole, or as a strategic priority. Rather, they are undertaken by individuals within the institution, often without recognition and in addition to their other (metricized) responsibilities.

The practices and qualities necessary to support universities in a transition toward becoming open knowledge institutions are progressive and forward looking. They involve a spectrum of activities that includes engaging with new communities and mediating new forms of conversation in order to engage new audiences and participants. These forward-facing practices are frequently at odds with the dominant, if unstated, expectations about what universities and colleges do, and who they are for.

Existing forms of evaluation generally reinforce dominant perspectives and power structures, including the geographic dominance of the Global North in traditional metrics. The conservative orientation of existing evaluation systems in universities today is further reinforced by the growth of external threats. Funding is tightening, and knowledge itself is increasingly politicized and contested. National and governmental goals can seem aligned with these agendas. This creates disincentives for experimentation and innovation in relation to collaboration beyond the institution, and can restrict new approaches to scholarly communication. Risk management favors conservatism. At the same time, open knowledge agendas offer a route to increasing the diversity of university funding and support sources as well as engaging with broader publics, including policy and opinion makers, and becoming part of a more collectively determined and knowledge-guided future.

Existing rankings and their relation to quality signaling are, of course, seen as crucial for universities and their administrators. Universities direct their knowledge and research output toward the defined set of activities and dissemination formats that feature in high-profile rankings. They do this in the hope of signaling status and prestige—and in so doing, ensuring their appeal to students and research funders. The exclusive use of specific data providers in some ranking systems can drive university policy to demand publication in specific—invariably traditional, Western, and science, technology, engineering, and mathematics–focused venues. One example is the use of Scopus data by the Times Higher Education World University Rankings. This narrows incentives for publication in formats and venues that might be more accessible to wider publics—for example, in scholar-led open-access journals, popular media, policy papers, or reports to the government. It also reinforces existing regional power hierarchies between the North and South as well as disciplinary divisions and practices. This in turn increases the ability of disciplines to enforce boundaries by determining what can and cannot be published within influential journals.

Efforts to prevent unfair comparisons when measuring the "reach and impact" of individual scholars and their work are problematic too. One illustration is the normalizing of citation scores with reference to an author's home discipline. These do not increase the fairness of the evaluation system. Rather, these strategies can themselves reinforce assumptions and biases, particularly for those conducting research across disciplinary boundaries. Even those within traditionally defined disciplines can be disadvantaged if they work in ways that do not conform to disciplinary norms. Work on issues considered to be local concerns by prestigious institutions, including, for instance, neglected tropical diseases, is often discounted. Activities involving mediation and communication are also frequently neglected, including the creative and performing arts along with many forms of research-led teaching and community engagement. This system of evaluation can especially push work directed at community building, including activities to support diversity, to the background or sometimes even underground.

Rankings create additional issues for universities with medium and lower world rankings that seek to distinguish themselves not by being the same as traditionally highly rated institutions but rather by being different. Creators of current ranking algorithms and reports are unlikely to either recognize or validate new measures that showcase differences to the advantage of these universities. The desire of such institutions to demonstrate their difference is thus countered by their simultaneous need to continue to place themselves as well as possible within existing ranking systems. Once again, this disadvantages many universities outside the traditional centers of academic power and prestige.

The homogenizing effect of rankings, and their perverse impacts on university strategies and decision making, pose a serious challenge to any effort to refine or redefine the role of a university or universities—including providing incentives for universities to change in ways that are congruent with the principles and protocols of OKIs.

Issues for Framework and Indicator Design

As suggested above, the aspects of an OKI that we have identified currently tend to be disregarded as valuable or measurable criteria within existing rankings and university evaluations. To some extent it might be argued that publication numbers or citations function as proxies for the mediation of knowledge. These numbers, however, have become so associated with concepts of "excellence" in university settings that they are now regarded as defining it. Their value as measures of knowledge mediation is questionable on two grounds: first, the limitations of citations in themselves as measures of any single quality, and second, the severely limited range of the users of research that citations report on. Other proxies that might have value for evaluating progress toward being an OKI have been investigated (e.g., via the EU Open Science Platform), but these are frequently limited in scope when compared to the ambition of the OKI agenda.

To avoid replicating past mistakes, an open knowledge framework must adhere to several principles:

- *Adaptability and like-to-like comparison*: Since the aim of a scoring system is to unify and compare across various entities, its framework (or underlying proxies) need to be flexible enough to adapt to different geographic settings in the target group. This is a particularly difficult challenge as institutions have vastly different management models, financial structures, student input, and so on. In situations where homogeneity is neither desired nor possible, classification and normalization systems should exist to allow like-to-like comparison.

- *Generalizability*: The test of a good indicator is the degree to which it serves as an adequate proxy for the underlying concept. For global indicators, it is important that the indicators represent the whole of the theoretical population in order to make inferences. For example, existing university rankings often fail to fully represent disciplines such as the humanities and social sciences, and research from the Global South is less likely to feature than that from the North. Global indicators must have global reach.

- *Standardization*: Several indicators/proxies can be imagined that demonstrate varying dimensions of openness. An open framework should be careful in standardization not to give undue priority to certain dimensions over others. Furthermore, it should avoid combining indicators where the underlying concept is not the same.

- *Orthogonality*: Information provided across various indicators is highly likely to overlap. Existing ranking systems frequently aggregate across such indicators without addressing this problem. Hence they create bias toward some criteria and undermine performance in other areas. A framework for open indicators should include a well-defined process for indicator selection, utilizing appropriate statistical procedures to ensure that the data underlying the indicators are as orthogonal as possible.

- *Qualitative versus quantitative data*: Qualitative data should not be neglected in favor of quantitative metrics. Although this complicates other aspects of the framework (e.g., standardization and generalization), a framework for open knowledge indicators must triangulate several sources of data to represent the complex and dynamic system of knowledge production.

- *Thoughtful design of scoring systems*: Another interesting and potentially important issue surrounds the way in which scores are assigned. Most current scoring systems utilize a bottom-to-top

scoring approach. This is where the baseline score for an indicator is zero and points are awarded according to activities signaling the desired outcome for the indicator. Khaki Sedigh (2017)
proposed an opposite approach where each indicator is assigned
a score of a hundred to start with and then points are deducted
for the lack of desired activities.

How Do Universities Change? Toward a Framework

In order to take practical steps toward transforming universities into
OKIs, we must acknowledge the ways in which current rankings
drive organizational change. This information needs to be used to
anticipate how openness can be introduced into existing rankings.
Comparison across institutions may be crucial to developing interest
in and momentum for system-wide changes. Any framework must
balance these needs, providing for the positive opportunities that
arise from competition and aspirational comparisons, while allowing an institution to follow its own path and local needs toward its
future.

There are three strands of evidence that we might use to evaluate a university. The first of these is evidence that a university is
developing and implementing policy that speaks to this overall
shift, whether in response to external pressure from government
and funders, from community or public demands, or internally.
Policy, strategy, and other public position statements are clearly not
a direct sign of change occurring, but they are a signal of intent as
well as proxy for organizational and institutional support of change.

The second strand of evidence emerges in the university's actions.
Is the institution putting in place platforms and systems that support
mediation, engagement, diversity, and network building? Is provision
for an institutional repository made and appropriately resourced?
Is there visible support for data management and sharing? Is there

support and expertise offered for crafting communications to speak with and effectively listen to appropriate communities?

The final strand will be evidence of outcomes and change. What evidence can we draw on as indicators or proxies of actual change? In some areas, such as assessing the degree of open access to formal traditional publications, this is becoming easier. As shown earlier, there has been a significant increase from many institutions over the past decade.

We can also see these three types of evidence as stages of development within a simple theory of change. In the first phase, characterized by policy development and deficit models, deficiencies are identified in specific areas of the university, and addressed by statements of intent or goals. In the second phase, there is action taken to address those deficiencies. Resource limitations will generally mean those actions are limited in scope, but well-designed actions and systems of resourcing will seek to maximize the positive benefits of these actions. The third stage is when outcomes result from actions, and ideally these are followed through evaluation and reflection, with new issues and unforeseen consequences identified, or limitations of the impacts of the actions taken.

A framework for open indicators should therefore include these three stages of development: policy and narrative signaling intent, action and investment that signals a prioritization of change, and measurable outcomes that result from these efforts.

Change is first propelled by an aspiration, often reflected in narrative or strategic documents or policy direction. This is generally driven by deficit models, where a problem is identified to be fixed. The second stage is action, which requires an investment of resources, time, money, or both. Choices here will be driven by investment models and identifying priorities. The final phase should deliver outcomes, and in an open knowledge system, these will be the subject of reflection and evaluation. Capacity models are appropriate to address the new capabilities and qualities of the university.

Aspiration	Action	Outcomes
(Policy/narrative)	(Investment)	(Evaluation)
Deficit models	Investment/priority models	Capacity models

Figure 8.1
A simple model of institutional change in universities.

Signals of Openness

A strong framework for open knowledge indicators requires the incorporation of many categories of information. Paramount to this is expanding the value proposition for research, not only by incentivizing publication in open-access venues, but investing in and rewarding work that is translational and focused on broader impacts beyond the research community. The way in which the campus engages with the outside community will be a major dimension of openness, which can be measured through active (e.g., partnerships) as well as more passive engagement (e.g., social media).

Investment in infrastructure is a key element in a strategy for openness. The creation of repositories is historically an element of openness, although a global connection of OKIs will give rise to fundamentally more advanced and expanded networked opportunities for making research available to other scholars and the public. The physical campus is also an element that can be investigated, looking at physical accessibility and spaces for open engagement.

Universities are centers of learning. Therefore openness will be evaluated in terms of the composition of the study body as well as the engagement in open educational activities (e.g., participation in online courses). At the institutional level, the university will be rewarded for the adoption of policies for openness, not unlike those established for journals such as the Transparency and Openness

Promotion Guidelines by the Center for Open Science (2015). These standards should seek to be comprehensive, not only incentivizing openness in one dimension of the university, but cutting across all university activities. Table 8.1 provides an illustration of potential data sources. This is not meant to be comprehensive but instead to provide examples of ways in which open knowledge indicators might be constructed.

A Proposal for an Evaluation Framework

Table 8.1 provides a large selection of potential signals and indicators of openness within universities. While there are a number of ways these could be characterized, we have found it most effective to use the three platforms or activities that we identified in chapters 3–4, and then explored in more detail in chapters 5–7. These categories—diversity, communication, and coordination—provide a convenient means of capturing all the signals and indicators in table 8.1.

They are also useful in that they correspond to existing external policy stimuli that universities are facing: the significant diversity and inclusion deficit that is a characteristic of most universities, and societal expectations to address those issues; the demands for open access, data, and methodology sharing usually seen under the banner of "open science"; and the broader demands for public engagement and inclusion in knowledge- and decision-making processes within society.

By combining the simple theory of change articulated earlier in this chapter with these three categories, we develop a framework that combines our categories of action with the processes by which change is implemented and evaluated. Each stage of development is characterized by specific types of instruments or actions, and this helps us to organize the relevant indicators. We do not at this

Table 8.1

Examples of Potential Indicators and Data Sources

Indicators	Data sources	Examples of cross-institution sources
Publications/data		
Open-access publications	Publication indexes and access data	Web of Science, Scopus, PubMed, Dimensions, Microsoft Academic, Unpaywall, DOAJ, BASE
Open-access repositories	Repository directories	Directory of Open Access Repositories (DOAR)
Open data	University repositories, community repositories/ indexes	DataCite, Figshare, Zenodo (but poor affiliation information)
Open data repositories	Registries	Registry of Research Data Repositories (re3data.org)
Open campus		
Open campus (physical/ online) accessibility, open events, massive open online courses [MOOCs], etc.)	Social media, library access and borrowing policies, MOOCs	MOOC Directory http://www.moocs.co/ MOOC List https://www .mooc-list.com/
Open education resources (OER)	Registries, world map	OER Policy Registry https://oerworldmap .org/oerpolicies, OER Commons https://www .oercommons.org/
Collaboration (academe, government, industry, etc.).	Higher education depart- ments, government reports	HERDC data (Australia)
Diversity		
Participation in education (student diversity)	Government statistical data, university websites, reporting frameworks	Athena SWAN status, HESA Statistics (UK), Department of Education, Skills and Employment (DESE), Higher Education Statistics (Australia)

(*continued*)

Table 8.1 (continued)

Examples of Potential Indicators and Data Sources

Indicators	Data sources	Examples of cross-institution sources
Participation as researchers and other staff (staff diversity)	Government statistical data, university websites, reporting frameworks	Gender Pay Gap reports (United Kingdom), Athena SWAN status (UK, Australia), Workplace Gender Equality Agency (United Kingdom, Australia), DESE Statistics (Australia), ETER, EUROSTAT (Europe), IPEDS (United States)
Output diversity	Authorship diversity, output type diversity, disciplinary diversity	CWTS Leiden Ranking, Crossref (output types)
Community engagement		
Participation by/in communities	University websites, event databases	Eventbrite
Investment in and priority given to research, translation, and communication	National and international networks	Research Impact, Development Research Uptake in Sub-Saharan Africa (DRUSSA), Learning Resource, Knowledge Translation Network Africa
Wider research impact	Impact reporting, altmetrics	REF United Kingdom Case Studies, altmetric.com, Crossref Event Data, PlumX
Standards		
University protocols for openness (e.g., open-access agreements or memoranda)	International agreements, university policies, individual statements, manifestos	Statements (e.g., Berlin Declaration, San Francisco Declaration on Research Assessment (DORA)
Investment in and adoption of open standards and protocols	University statements, public budget documents	
Strategic planning toward openness and integration into all university operations	University budget / annual reports, funding for open access	

stage seek to refine these into any quantitative system of evaluation but instead present the framework as a way of identifying areas for evaluation as well as identifying gaps in our current information landscape.

One particular objection to this framework might be that action frequently precedes policy and organizational statements. Individuals will often be acting, sometimes without organizational sanction, to pursue an open agenda. Such activities are not organizational, however, precisely because they are not incorporated into the organizational narrative. The principle of subsidiarity supports the development of these local initiatives in the sense that it seeks to create an environment in which they are not prevented, but until they are adopted by the organization, they do not signal organizational activity. They are not yet institutionalized.

Institutionalizing Open Knowledge

In table 8.2 above there is a challenge as we move from left to right. It becomes increasingly difficult to know in which row a particular signal belongs. This problem actually points us toward a more rigorous theory of change that maps well onto the models that we develop in chapter 3. When we start on the journey of change, we will naturally engage with deficit models. What are we *not* doing? What do we need to *change* or do *better*? Policy efforts respond by targeting specific areas, ideally with as much focus as possible. Open-access policies never seem to address issues of diversity and inclusion, and diversity policies rarely, if ever, mention open access. But we cannot achieve the aspirations of open access in delivering more *usable* research outputs unless we address how our communications are currently affected by the lack of diversity in the academy. If we aim to communicate more effectively to diverse communities, then we need to include the experience of those diverse communities

Table 8.2

A Framework for Organizing the Evaluation of Universities as OKIs

	Aspiration (Policy/narrative)	Action (Investment)	Outcomes (Evaluation)
Diversity	Diversity and inclusion policy	Engagement with diversity programs	Staff/student diversity
	Policy on communications and evaluation (output diversity)	Staffing and support	Underrepresented minority retention statistics
		Training programs	
		Interdisciplinary programs	Diversity of revenue sources
	Public engagement/comms policy		Output (format) diversity
Coordination	Library access policies	Investment in public transport integration/civil provisioning	Attendance at public events
	Campus planning and public access		Collaboration measures
	Policy support for coordination and/or community building	Support for public events	Public engagement/citizen science measures
Communication	Open-access policy	Open-access funding	Percent of open-access outputs
	Data management policy	Data management and repository support	Data shared and archived
	Public engagement/comms policy		Public access of outputs
	Communication in core documents	Support for wider communications	Public engagement

within the process of building that knowledge and planning its communication.

The consideration of how these different areas relate to each comes into focus when we move to the next phase of our theory of change. As soon as a university invests resources, whether time or money, there are choices to be made about where those resources are deployed. Do you invest in paying article processing charges to deliver open access or is that money better spent on childcare provision? While this may appear a contrived example, these choices are often made implicitly and without consideration of an overall strategy. Katie Wilson and colleagues (2019) point out how those universities that perform well on open access to formal research outputs are not strongly correlated with universities that provide greater public access to the physical resources their libraries hold, illustrating a potential gap in the strategic thinking around information access.

How do universities need to change so as to find synergies between these investments? How can supporting the public to physically enter a library enhance their access to the digital open-access outputs of the university? How might investment in childcare also provide a connection to user communities for relevant research? How does the provision of support for open access and childcare build and strengthen those connections?

Policy and aspiration usually address single areas for change and not the combination. When investments are made, priorities need to be set. The systems for decision making contribute to the process of cultural and institutional change. A fully functioning OKI will have cultural and institutional forms that work to hold the three areas in tension, providing an optimal (but probably not the globally optimal) outcome for the organization in its current environment.

This leads us to the final phase. An imagined organization where it is the culture and institutional forms that hold all these issues in tension. There is no correct solution, but rather behaviors and practices that help to optimize the overall position as a whole. Just as in chapter 3 we talk about a shift in that optimum as a result of societal and technological change, we see here how culture and institutions (in the political economy sense) need to build and sustain that work to hold these conflicting requirements in tension.

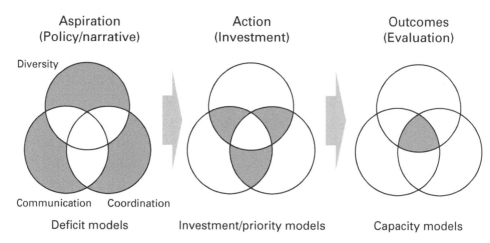

Figure 8.2
The journey toward an OKI.

The key questions we need to ask therefore are how policy, investment, internal evaluation, and environmental change are contributing to this institution and culture building? How is this complex of competing factors being harnessed toward those goals? What works? What does not? This places evaluation firmly within the process of change, but also illustrates how on its own—as with policy making and investment—it is not enough.

A Forward-Looking and Open Framework

Most existing evaluation frameworks for institutions today look backward, based on the reporting of a limited set of outputs. Here we want to assess the orientation of a university to an unknown future, where new communities are engaged in ways that are difficult to predict. The explicit challenge to doing so is that any fixed framework for evaluation will be inherently conservative.

There is much interest in predictive analytics of academic work, but there is also little evidence that these do more than reinforce existing power structures, rents, and inequities. Systems based on predicting future performance, with a focus on present obsessions, from currently available data that are based on trajectories of success from the past, do little to help us challenge and diversify existing systems along with their closed nature.

If we only examine those instances of success found in our own local traditions, we can easily miss developments in other spaces and systems. The examples of Action Dialogues in South Africa have already been discussed. Another illustration includes SciELO, the open-access publishing platform in Latin America, although it remains relatively unknown outside South America and southern Africa. More than that, many of the activities and practices that align with OKIs may be deliberately hidden within the institution, operating under the radar to avoid scrutiny based on more traditional objectives.

We will need to identify institutions that bring those activities to the forefront, both locally and more widely. We will need a model that helps us identify the signals that an institution is supporting these activities. This framework is only a start along that journey. It needs to be open in itself, and any implementation that is applied to evaluation needs to allow for new signals or more relevant information to be added where appropriate.

If a path toward becoming an OKI can only be discovered step by step, then no single framework can provide simply evaluative answers. Equally there is the potential for a diversity of paths and universities in a diversity of contexts. This does not mean that evaluation is impossible, nor that progress on a selected set of indicators is not valuable. It simply means that the selection of indicators will be dependent on context as well as the goals and values of each institution.

A framework can supply a means of aiding the process of indicator selection. It can even help in comparing and contrasting the progress of different institutions. In this sense our work aligns with best practice efforts such as Research Quality Plus developed by the Canadian International Development Research Center (2018; Lebel and McLean 2018), HuMetricsHSS (n.d.) project, and European Expert Group on Indicators for Open Science (Schomberg et al. 2020). All these focus on the role of frameworks in guiding the selection of indicators for specific evaluations.

OKIs evolve over time, and their evaluation approaches must evolve with them. A commitment to openness, a state of poise between chaos and control, requires constant calibration and reevaluation—not least in the processes of calibration and evaluation themselves. It is not possible to achieve openness by measuring it in a closed way.

9
Action

Ways Forward: Technical, Political, or Both?

The pathways to an open knowledge society must navigate between the two extremes of chaos or anarchy, and order or control. These dystopic extremes attract different characteristic forms. At the "chaos" end of the spectrum are clustered libertarian and anarchic solutions. This is where you'll find the "global technofix," which follows the Silicon Valley model of innovation. At the "control" end of the spectrum are clustered authoritarian, "command-and-control," and rule-governed solutions, which governments themselves will tend toward. In other words, the two extremes are both dystopic, each in its own way. Total chaos or total control are equally destructive, without securing a "poised system," as Stuart Kauffman (1991) put it, that can self-regulate as well as adapt to difference, newness, and change.

The urge to openness is itself a by-product of the technological fix culture. It became a buzzword of the 2010s, prompting professional skeptic Evgeny Morozov (2013a) to call a halt: "'Openness' has become a dangerously vague term, with lots of sex appeal but barely any analytical content. Certified as 'open,' the most heinous and suspicious ideas suddenly become acceptable."

Morozov distinguishes between different kinds of openness—for example, Karl Popper's "open society," which is a political argument for the free flow of ideas in a democratic polity, and "open-source" computation, which is an engineering fix for the greater efficiency of technical innovation. Apply the engineering fix to the political problem and "a victory for 'openness' might also signify defeat for democratic politics, ambitious policy reform and much else," he wrote in the *New York Times*. Conversely, "ambitious policy reform" without "openness" to accountability can result in suboptimal outcomes, when political agendas are driven by backroom policy advisers and lobbyists (Morozov (2013a). Even elective democratic politics can weaponize "openness" when the concept is captured by populists and authoritarians (see Worthy and Heide 2019).

Technofix

One way to ensure open knowledge is the technofix: leave knowledge production, management, and distribution to Silicon Valley and its venture capitalist–driven entrepreneurial endeavors in protocol making, company start-ups, infrastructure building, and app development. This method certainly produces technological "solutionism" (Morozov 2013b), and has populated and nourished the global commercial internet since the 1990s. Advocates for distributed ledger, or blockchain technologies, as the next generation of the internet argue that it will provide an information platform that is fast, instantly global, and free of central control at a structural level. There are early indications that this is a direction in which policy trends are heading (e.g., Novak 2019; Hughes et al. 2019; Organization for Economic Cooperation and Development 2019).

There is certainly cause for optimism here, as the latter is also the model of Wikipedia and open-source software, in both of which a globally distributed group of people has been able to organize and technofix production around a protocol for developing a common pool resource. But in many ways, Wikipedia and open-source software, while mostly well-governed organizational forms, can also illustrate the deeper problems of anarchy and lurking dystopia endemic to the technofix model.

The problem with the technofix to the open knowledge problem is that while conforming to the "better-faster-cheaper" model of tech progress, on some of the margins it tends toward the anarchy end of the spectrum, risking problems of loss of control. Without public oversight and control, therefore, issues of access injustice, privacy violations, and arbitrary and dangerous interventions become inevitable. Open knowledge constructed in institutions such as these risks disappearing into the "dark web" beyond moderators and oversight, and becoming uncensorable and uncontrollable.

The private provision of public infrastructure comes with costs too, such as for consumers, when "private" comes to mean "what the market we control will bear" rather than "what competitive provision may cost" (e.g., health care in the United States and private schools everywhere). As a result of these developments, there are also costs imposed on the disruption to established business models. This potentially applies to the accrued benefits of settled ways of doing things, for institutions such as libraries, publishers, and funders that have thus far adapted to a settled regime of public funding of closed knowledge production.

Another problem with technofix is the culture that it supports, where computational and engineering skills outcompete social and human skills. Not only does this lead to "solutions" skewed in favor of tech corporations, but it permits and encourages a working environment where sexual, ethnic, and social diversity are actively harassed (Cook 2020):

> Silicon Valley consistently embeds its values—as White and upwardly mobile—into the architecture of its products, many of which have come under fire as racist, and extend into its business and hiring practices. By ignoring issues of race (and, likewise, issues of class, gender and sexual identity) by gesturing to them as

being old economy problems, they circumvent any meaningful interventions that work toward dismantling of barriers based on them, and reinscribe longstanding discriminatory practices. (Noble and Roberts 2019, 16)

Political Fix

The other way to solve the problem of open knowledge is through politics, which can tend toward dystopia in a different way. Proposed solutions tend to use political mechanisms to force collective action, adding oversight and enforcement to aspects of the business process, such as funding shares, intellectual property transfer agreements, access, and censorship prospects. This is the control end of the spectrum. It has the advantage of using elective and representative mechanisms, but "politics as usual"—a sclerotic social institution—also needs to reform its own knowledge systems and sources. Informed civic leadership is as important as community participation in order to maintain deliberative independence from business and other pressures, update public policy on taxation, energy (climate justice), regulation, and welfare (post–COVID-19), and adapt policy to changing technological, global, digital, and creative realities (Bernhard et al. 2020).

While "politics" remains confined to narrow specialist professionals (and vulnerable to putsch by determined ideological groups), there is little chance of recasting represented populations from consumer-spectators to citizen-cocreators. If the aim of politics remains self-interest (and winner takes all), it is hard to build a broad-based "innovation commons" (Potts 2019). But if the goal of politics is to broaden the base of knowledgeable cooperation for regenerative communal sustainability (Keane 2018), then citizenship becomes a serious matter of "open" self-organization for the transformation of both productive and social systems.

The dystopic aspects here include the use of political power and force (rather than voluntary action) to create an outcome. And because this is a negotiated process whose outcome depends on who is at the table, some will be left out, creating new divides and the potential exclusion of those who are not part of the political process. This tendency is already visible in various attempts made and measures taken by a variety of national governments in order to enforce national control and borders on the internet, resulting in reduced access by national research communities to open information.

The institutional political process inevitably draws in the same actors, and will tend toward replicating and reinforcing the patterns of past decisions, as it works through the same channels and mechanisms of power. Even with the best intentions and brightest political agents, the process will be slow and conservative (but see Thunberg 2019).

Toward an Inclusive Institutionalization of Open Knowledge

Eutopia in the space of OKIs is not a rejection of the technofix or political control agenda but instead an attempt to find and embed the best aspects of both, and shed the worst aspects of the existing systems. This is a work of synthesis, integration, and system evolution, not one of invention or destruction.

We seek a good solution that will put structure into our technical undertakings, and recognizes the critical need for inclusive (diverse) and participatory (structured process) governance systems. So we need negotiated protocols. The technofix is needed for the efficiencies and new affordances it brings. But political control via knowledge-rich institutional processes is also needed to create a fair and representative system.

An open knowledge system, in the "narrow range for eutopia" vision, has complex institutional characteristics and practical outcomes that mix the best aspects of the technofix and negotiated political settlement. We will recognize a poised OKI by its characteristics and properties, which will vary according to context and situation as well as purpose.

An open knowledge system will open more knowledge for more people than a closed one. That offers a powerful productive potential as well as highly desirable outcomes in relation to the diversity and inclusion that are baked into the open approach. An open knowledge system naturally produces different forms and sources of knowledge. These qualities of abundance and social justice need to be set against the other key aspect of an open knowledge system as a complex institutional space and site for "staged conflict" (Hartley 2018).

To build such a knowledge institution with complex dynamic properties requires the mixing of technology and protocol-driven infrastructure with consensus-driven negotiations (see Poppe, Leininger, and Wolff 2019). The end result, ideally, will be poised in adaptive tension between the opposing poles of too much chaos and too much order.

OKIs facilitate participation rather than adopting top-down, controlling, and exclusive approaches. This coordination process seeks to establish productive and collaborative linkages with a variety of actors and stakeholders, and between the grass roots and initiatives in the realm of external regulators.

Inclusive coordination not only provides platforms for dialogue among participants but imagines permeability among types of knowledge participants too. That is, an OKI takes for granted that a knowledge "consumer" is also a user and advocate, and a beneficiary is a maker. Where all such roles are valued (i.e., where citizens are not reduced to consumers), open possibilities for the simultaneous and sequential embodiment in various roles can be maintained. Furthermore, it must be recognized that the system of knowledge production comprises many competing value systems. For example, an institution may be subject to certain regulatory frameworks that might not apply to a knowledge maker. In turn, the knowledge maker may be responding to disciplinary pressures that are external to the institution. Coordination requires awareness of and attention to these competing priority and value systems. Subsidiarity only works if difference is "owned" by those who meet and work across otherwise conflicted boundaries.

There are strong parallels here with what Kathleen Fitzpatrick describes as "generous thinking" in her book of that name. Fitzpatrick (2019, 209) makes the distinction between "caring about"—a performative statement of values—and "caring for," an active commitment to an ethical stance of care for people and communities. Her rich conceptualization of "generosity" can be seen as a parallel process to our goal of articulating what we mean by "openness." The differences between approaches lies in Fitzpatrick's focus on the agency of the moral individual to act, and our focus on the institution. As Fitzpatrick (2020) observes, "And I also know that however much I may want to keep the institution running, the institution is not thinking the same about me. Our institutions will not, cannot, love us back. However much we sacrifice for them, they cannot, will not, sacrifice for us."

Where Fitzpatrick asserts that the institution itself cannot care "for," we would argue that it must. The culture, standards, systems, and economies of the institution as well as the university must guide its members toward both individual generosity and institutional openness. This is necessarily the work of the privileged. A truly open institution must not just be working to address Tressie McMillan Cottom's criticism, as quoted by Fitzpatrick (2020): "I don't think these institutions can support us or love us. And I honor the many people who work to make them more humane. But you, alone, can not do that. And you cannot do it, ever, by killing yourself." Those with the capacity and power must actively and continuously work to institutionalize a culture and system in which addressing those issues is seen as valuable and important work, both by encouraging the privileged to do this work, and also by *institutionally* valuing the contributions and criticisms that only those with the experience of bias and exclusion can bring.

Sensitive coordination will always maintain a precarious balance between empowerment and control. As noted earlier, actors within a knowledge system are subject to differing pressures and regulation. To attend to these pressures, coordination must ensure maximum flexibility while meeting the needs of accountability bodies and regulatory agencies. Coordination of an open system, furthermore, requires certain sensitivities to potential countercurrents. Given that systems may evolve to a closed state, effective mechanisms must be in place to incentivize and reward openness.

Ways to Proceed

Our goal is a university that engages deeply with the mission of an OKI by drawing on the values, structures, and activities of open knowledge, and including them into its organizational and community story. Such an open institution provides a platform for distributed innovation and maximal impact.

Within this broad framework, there is also the need for monitoring and self-regulation at the institutional level for a university to decide how to assess its own progress. Although established frameworks for measuring the effectiveness of universities in traditional terms are a reality, OKIs have the courage and ability to contribute to change in the ways that universities are positioned and understood, internally and externally.

In turn, this suggests that OKIs will need to be supported by guidance and best practice protocols. This support might take the form of possible models, best practice, and cautionary tales of common mistakes, alongside advice on how other organizations have decided to represent their own progress.

We intend this book to be a first step in the development of a framework to guide action and illustrate pathways forward.

Leading the Way

In a complex evolutionary pathway toward OKIs, leadership matters. Some must go first. Leaders can be individuals, groups, and organizations. They can emerge in all kinds of contexts:

- *The government*, apart from being the regulator, can support the transition in many ways as a leader. Open access can be included systematically as a requirement for government-funded research. Public universities may pay special attention to increasing the inclusiveness of their staff and student body, and be rewarded accordingly. In the polarity between technofix and political fix, governments can take an active role in mediating and moderating negotiations between business and universities in creating common knowledge pools.

- *Professional associations* play an essential role in leading the process of overhauling the dominant system of journal rankings, peer review procedures, and performance evaluation of academics. They can actively support and honor cross-disciplinary research initiatives via the creation of new venues for publishing innovative research.

- *Scientific and scholarly publishers* can create innovative ways to combine commercial interests with maximizing open access, and may actively pursue cooperation with other concerned parties such as professional associations.

- *Universities* can overhaul their systems of selecting and evaluating faculty and staff, thereby changing the incentives for teachers and researchers. They can reward all kinds of common knowledge pools that transcend the boundaries of established approaches such as community projects.

- *Researchers* can take the lead as open knowledge entrepreneurs, taking the risk in exploring new common knowledge pools. Senior researchers may actively support new open-access journals by redirecting their submissions away from the incumbents.

- *Teachers* can develop new curricula in keeping with the more open nature of knowledge and growing diversity of university populations.
- *Students* can be presented with real options within and between universities, including those that model open knowledge initiatives, and students can organize activism for openness.
- *Funders* can include open knowledge criteria in their project selection and evaluation procedures. They can identify emerging common knowledge pools, moving away from narrow criteria of excellence, for example, by widening the peer and expert review system to include other concerned parties.
- *Professions* can actively cooperate with universities in creating programs that integrate knowledge users in their design and implementation. They can support research initiatives that bridge research and application.
- *Communities* can actively support spatial integration between universities and localities. They can approach universities with cultural and other community projects, acting as local knowledge entrepreneurs.
- *International organizations* can develop blueprints for open knowledge initiatives. They can lend active support to developing countries in building new OKIs and act as mediators across national policies.
- *Standards setters* can actively support the increasing openness of standards globally.

Amid all this opportunity, there is a place for all.

Key Terms

This is not an exhaustive glossary of technical definitions but instead a brief recap of how various key terms are used within this book.

- **Club good**: An economic good that is nonrivalrous but excludable. Also known as "toll goods." Club goods do not experience market failure and are often efficiently privately provided *local public goods*.

- **Common pool resource**: An economic good that is rivalrous but nonexcludable. Requires governance. Fisheries and forests are classic examples. Elinor Ostrom (1990) showed that neither the state nor markets can effectively supply common pool resources, and that under certain circumstances, they are efficiently managed by communities.

- **Diversity**: A general property of difference within systems.

- **Evaluation**: A process in which a system is compared to some form of benchmark that may be internal or external, and qualitative or quantitative. We are particularly interested in helping universities evaluate, in as self-critical and objective a manner as possible, their progress toward an imagined future as OKIs.

- **High-ranking bureaucrat**: You know who you are. You know what you have to do.

- **Indicator**: A data point that can be associated with an aspect of interest in a system. Qualitative or quantitative in form. Indicators are to be contrasted with metrics, which are connected to a rigorous theory of measurement, and proxies, which are data that are usefully associated with and may be predictive of an aspect of interest, but for which there is no theoretical connection.

- **Open access**: Has various contested technical definitions. It is used here in a generic sense of scholarly objects that can be freely accessed online without charge and with no restrictions beyond those inherent in gaining access to network infrastructures.

- **Open knowledge institution**: An institution (below) that solves one or more of the collective action problems involved in producing knowledge as a common pool resource.

  ○ **Open**: Free from restrictions. Not used here in any of the formal (but limited!) open-source, free software, or open knowledge definition, and not limited to copyrightable objects. Can be applied to objects, processes, communities, and systems.

  ○ **Knowledge**: Useful understandings of the world. Contextual and bound. Effort is required to move and translate knowledge to different contexts.

  ○ **Institution**: Rules for coordination. Not a synonym for "a legal entity" or "long-standing organization."

- **Organization**: A legal entity or clearly defined ordering (usually hierarchical) of agents for some purpose. An organization is not an institution.

- **Penguin**: A flightless aquatic bird of the family *Spheniscidae* including the modern genera *Aptenodytes*, *Eudyptes*, *Eudyptula*, *Megadyptes*, *Pygoscelis*, and *Spheniscus*. Penguins live exclusively in the Southern Hemisphere. They really like to eat fish and are surprisingly graceful in the water, yet not on land. Also (aka Penguin Books), a book publisher founded by Allen Lane, based largely in the Northern Hemisphere.

- **Private good**: An economic good that is excludable and rivalrous. Efficiently provided by firms and markets.

- **Public good**: A economic good that is nonexcludable and nonrivalrous. That is, it is difficult to prevent others using it and can be distributed without loss. Public goods experience market failure and are efficiently supplied by governments. Not used in this book in the sense of "the public interest."

- **Public interest**: That which is good for the public, as judged by elites (or when those elites are economists, a *social welfare function*). "*The* public good" (politics) is commonly but mistakenly confused with "*a* public good" (economics).

- **Subsidiarity**: Subsidiarity is the principle that responsibility for decisions and actions resides as close as possible to the makers of knowledge—that is, at the lowest possible point in an administrative hierarchy.

- **University**: Used in a broad sense to include liberal arts colleges, research, and teaching organizations. In some countries, the university is defined in law.

References

Advance HE. 2020. Review of the Athena SWAN Charter. https://www.ecu.ac.uk/equality-charters/athena-swan/review-of-the-athena-swan-charter/.

Advance HE. n.d. About Advance HE's Athena SWAN Charter. Accessed May 1, 2020. https://www.ecu.ac.uk/equality-charters/athena-swan/about-athena-swan/.

Aghazadeh, Sarah A., Alison Burns, Jun Chu, Hazel Feigenblatt, Elizabeth Laribee, Lucy Maynard, Amy L. M. Meyers, Jessica L. O'Brien, and Leah Rufus. 2018. GamerGate: A Case Study in Online Harassment. In *Online Harassment*, edited by Jennifer Golbeck, 179–207. Human–Computer Interaction Series. Cham, Switzerland: Springer International Publishing. https://doi.org/10.1007/978-3-319-78583-7_8.

Allen, Darcy W. E., Chris Berg, Brendan Markey-Towler, Mikayla Novak, and Jason Potts. 2020. Blockchain and the Evolution of Institutional Technologies: Implications for Innovation Policy. *Research Policy* 49 (1): 103865. https://doi.org/10.1016/j.respol.2019.103865.

Alper, Alexandra. 2020. Chinese Envoy Takes Veiled Swipe at Trump for Politicising Coronavirus. *Sydney Morning Herald*, April 21, North America sec. https://www.smh.com.au/world/north-america/chinese-envoy-takes-veiled-swipe-at-trump-for-politicising-coronavirus-20200422-p54m07.html.

Ball, Joanna, and Graham Stone. 2019. Opening up the Library: Transforming Our Structures, Policies and Practices. Paper presented at LIBER 2019, Dublin, Ireland. https://zenodo.org/record/3260298#.XwM1_S9q2fA.

Barnett, Antony. 2001. Pharmaceutical Firms Plunder Africa's Native Lore. *Guardian*, June 17. https://www.theguardian.com/world/2001/jun/17/inter nationaleducationnews.businessofresearch.

Bernhard, Michael, Allen Hicken, Christopher Reenock, and Staffan I. Lindberg. 2020. Parties, Civil Society, and the Deterrence of Democratic Defection. *Studies in Comparative International Development* 55 (1): 1–26. https://doi.org/10.1007/s12116-019-09295-0.

Bhopal, Kalwant, and Holly Henderson. 2019. Advancing Equality in Higher Education: An Exploratory Study of the Athena SWAN and Race Equality Charters. Birmingham, UK: University of Birmingham. https://www .birmingham.ac.uk/research/crre/research/advancing-equality-in-higher -education.aspx.

Bilder, Geoffrey. 2016. The Citation Fetish. https://doi.org/10.6084/m9 .figshare.3501629.v1.

Boberg, Svenja, Thorsten Quandt, Tim Schatto-Eckrodt, and Lena Frischlich. 2020. Pandemic Populism: Facebook Pages of Alternative News Media and the Corona Crisis—a Computational Content Analysis. *ArXiv:2004.02566 [Cs]*, April. http://arxiv.org/abs/2004.02566.

Boboltz, Sara. 2015. Editors Are Trying to Fix Wikipedia's Gender and Racial Bias Problem. *HuffPost Canada*, April 15. https://www.huffpost.com /entry/wikipedia-gender-racial-bias_n_7054550.

Bogle, Ariel. 2017. Australian Research "Has a Diversity Problem." *ABC News*, November 24. https://www.abc.net.au/news/science/2017-11-24/australian -research-has-a-daversity-problem/9178786.

Brazilian Forum of Public Health Journals Editors and Associação Brasileira de Saúde Coletiva. 2015. Motion to Repudiate Mr. Jeffrey Beall's Classist Attack on SciELO. *SciELO in Perspective* (blog), August 2. https://blog.scielo .org/en/2015/08/02/motion-to-repudiate-mr-jeffrey-bealls-classist-attack -on-scielo/#.XnxE71BS-3c.

Brembs, Björn. 2016. Data Show "Excellence Initiative" Was a Massive Failure—Help Stop It. *Bjoern.Brembs.Blog* (blog), April 28. http://bjoern .brembs.net/2016/04/data-show-excellence-initiative-was-a-massive -failure-help-stop-it/.

Center for Open Science. 2015. Transparency and Openness Promotion Guidelines. 2015. https://www.cos.io/top.

Chan, Leslie, Darius Cuplinskas, Michael Eisen, Fred Friend, Yana Genova, Jean-Claude Guédon, Melissa Hagemann, et al. 2002. Budapest Open Access. http://www.budapestopenaccessinitiative.org/read.

Chinese National Knowledge Infrastructure Network. n.d. Accessed March 26, 2020. http://www.cnki.net/.

Collins, Harry. 2010. *Tacit and Explicit Knowledge*. Chicago: University of Chicago Press.

Cook, Katy. 2020. *The Psychology of Silicon Valley: Ethical Threats and Emotional Unintelligence in the Tech Industry*. London: Palgrave Macmillan. http://library.oapen.org/bitstream/handle/20.500.12657/22851/1007310.pdf.

Costa Maia, Leonor, Ana Odete Santos Vieira, Ariana Luna Peixoto, João Renato Stehmann, Maria Regina de Vasconcellos Barbosa, and Mariângela Menezes. 2017. Construindo redes para promover o conhecimento da biodiversidade brasileira: a experiência do INCT—Herbário Virtual. [Building networks to promote knowledge of Brazil's: The experience of the INCT—Virtual Herbarium]. Campinas, Brazil: Instituto Nacional de Ciência e Tecnologia (INCT)—Herbário Virtual da Flora e dos Fungos. http://inct.florabrasil.net/wp-content/uploads/2017/08/inct_livro_10_2_ed-online.pdf.

Creative Commons. 2017. State of the Commons 2017. https://stateof.creativecommons.org.

Creative Commons. 2019a. Creative Commons Licenses. https://creativecommons.org/use-remix/cc-licenses/.

Creative Commons. 2019b. What We Do. https://creativecommons.org/about/.

Creative Commons. n.d. What's New in 4.0. Accessed May 4, 2020. https://creativecommons.org/version4/.

Creative Commons Global Network. n.d. About. Accessed May 30, 2020. https://network.creativecommons.org/about/.

DFG, German Research Foundation. 2020. Excellence Strategy. https://www.dfg.de/en/research_funding/programmes/excellence_strategy/index.html.

Djankov, Simeon, Edward Glaeser, Rafael La Porta, Florencio Lopez-de-Silanes, and Andrei Shleifer. 2003. The New Comparative Economics. *Journal of Comparative Economics* 31 (4): 595–619. https://doi.org/10.1016/j.jce.2003.08.005.

Donoghue, Frank. 2008. *The Last Professors: The Corporate University and the Fate of the Humanities*. New York: Fordham University Press.

DW (Deutsche Welle). 2020. "Pandemic Populism": Germany Sees Rise in Conspiracy Theories. April 26. https://www.dw.com/en/pandemic-populism-germany-sees-rise-in-conspiracy-theories/a-53240063.

Extance, Andy. 2017. Could Bitcoin Technology Help Science? *Nature* 552 (7685): 301–302.

Fecher, Benedikt, and Sascha Friesike. 2014. Open Science: One Term, Five Schools of Thought. In *Opening Science: The Evolving Guide on How the Internet Is Changing Research, Collaboration, and Scholarly Publishing*, edited by Sönke Bartling and Sascha Friesike, 17–47. Cham, Switzerland: Springer International Publishing. https://doi.org/10.1007/978-3-319-00026-8_2.

Felski, Rita. 1989. *Beyond Feminist Aesthetics: Feminist Literature and Social Change*. Cambridge, MA: Harvard University Press.

Fitzpatrick, Kathleen. 2019. *Generous Thinking: A Radical Approach to Saving the University*. Baltimore: Johns Hopkins University Press.

Fitzpatrick, Kathleen. 2020. Generosity in Hard Times. *Kathleen Fitzpatrick* (blog), April 26. https://kfitz.info/generosity-in-hard-times/.

Freeman, Jo. n.d. The Tyranny of Stucturelessness. Jo Freeman.com. Accessed May 4, 2020. https://www.jofreeman.com/joreen/tyranny.htm.

Freunde von GISAID e.V. 2020. GISAID—Initiative. https://www.gisaid.org/.

Gan, Nectar, Caitlin Hu, and Ivan Watson. 2020. Beijing Tightens Grip over Coronavirus Research amid US-China Row on Virus Origin. *CNN*, April 16. https://edition.cnn.com/2020/04/12/asia/china-coronavirus-research-restrictions-intl-hnk/index.html.

Gardenswartz, Lee, Anita Rowe, Patricia Digh, and Martin Bennett. 2003. *The Global Diversity Desk Reference: Managing an International Workforce*. San Francisco: Pfeiffer.

Gardner, Sue. 2011. Nine Reasons Women Don't Edit Wikipedia (in Their Own Words). *Sue Gardner's Blog* (blog), February 20. https://suegardner.org/2011/02/19/nine-reasons-why-women-dont-edit-wikipedia-in-their-own-words/.

Garfield, Eugene. 2006. The History and Meaning of the Journal Impact Factor. *Journal of the American Medical Association* 295 (1): 90. https://doi.org/10.1001/jama.295.1.90.

Habgood-Coote, Joshua. 2019. Stop Talking about Fake News! *Inquiry* 62 (9–10): 1033–1065. https://doi.org/10.1080/0020174X.2018.1508363.

Harmsworth, Garth, Shaun Awatere, and Mahuru Robb. 2016. Indigenous Māori Values and Perspectives to Inform Freshwater Management in Aotearoa-New Zealand. *Ecology and Society* 21 (4): article 19. https://doi.org /10.5751/ES-08804-210409.

Hartley, John. 2018. What Hope for Open Knowledge? Productive (Armed) vs. Connective (Tribal) Knowledge and Staged Conflict. *Cultural Science* 10 (1): 27–41. https://doi.org/10.5334/csci.107.

Hartley, John, W. Wen, and Henry Li. 2015. *Creative Economy and Culture.* London: Sage Publications.

Harvard University Endowment. 2020. Wikipedia. https://en.wikipedia.org /w/index.php?title=Harvard_University_endowment&oldid=952616575.

Haupt, Adam. 2014. *Hip-Hop Activism in Post-Apartheid South Africa.* UCT Summer School Lectures, University of Cape Town. https://open.uct.ac.za /handle/11427/7728.

Heimstädt, Maximilian. 2020. Between Fast Science and Fake News: Preprint Servers Are Political. *Impact of Social Sciences* (blog), April 3. https:// blogs.lse.ac.uk/impactofsocialsciences/2020/04/03/between-fast-science -and-fake-news-preprint-servers-are-political/.

Henderson, Matthew, Alan Mendoza, Andrew Foxall, James Rogers, and Sam Armstrong. 2020. Coronavirus Compensation? Assessing China's Potential Culpability and Avenues of Legal Response. Henry Jackson Society. April 5. https://henryjacksonsociety.org/publications/coronaviruscompensation/.

Hess, Charlotte, and Elinor Ostrom. 2006. A Framework for Analysing the Microbiological Commons. *International Social Science Journal* 58 (188): 335–349. https://doi.org/10.1111/j.1468-2451.2006.00622.x.

Holmström, Bengt. 2017. Pay for Performance and Beyond. *American Economic Review* 107 (7): 1753–1777. https://doi.org/10.1257/aer.107.7.1753.

Hughes, Laurie, Yogesh K. Dwivedi, Santosh K. Misra, Nripendra P. Rana, Vishnupriya Raghavan, and Viswanadh Akella. 2019. Blockchain Research, Practice and Policy: Applications, Benefits, Limitations, Emerging Research Themes and Research Agenda. *International Journal of Information Management* 49 (December): 114–129. https://doi.org/10.1016/j.ijinfomgt.2019.02.005.

HuMetricsHSS. n.d. About HuMetricsHSS. Accessed May 4, 2020. http:// humetricshss.org/about/.

IFLA. 2015. IFLA Statement on Libraries and Intellectual Freedom. https:// www.ifla.org/publications/ifla-statement-on-libraries-and-intellectual -freedom.

International Research Development Center. 2018. Research Quality Plus. June 14. https://www.idrc.ca/en/research-in-action/research-quality-plus.

JISC. n.d. Welcome to OpenDOAR—v2. Sherpa. JISC Digital Resources Open Access. Accessed May 4, 2020. https://v2.sherpa.ac.uk/opendoar/.

Johns Hopkins University Press. 2019. History. https://www.press.jhu.edu /about/history.

Journal of Open Source Software. n.d. Accessed May 1, 2020. https://joss.theoj .org.

Katz, Daniel S. 2019. Second Thoughts on Proper Citation Guidance for Software Developers. *Daniel S. Katz's Blog* (blog), December 20. https:// danielskatzblog.wordpress.com/2019/12/20/thoughts-on-citation-guid ance-for-developers/.

Kauffman, Stuart A. 1991. Antichaos and Adaptation. *Scientific American* 265 (2): 78–85.

Kauffman, Stuart A. 1993. *The Origins of Order: Self-Organization and Selection in Evolution.* New York: Oxford University Press.

Keane, John. 2018. *Power and Humility: The Future of Monitory Democracy.* Cambridge: Cambridge University Press.

Kelly, Kevin. 2015. My New Book The Inevitable Will Appear in Chinese First. It Went on Presale Today in China and Sold 20,000 Copies in the First 2 Hours! Twitter, 2:50 a.m., November 6. https://twitter.com/kevin2kelly /status/662582744896045056?lang=en.

Khaki Sedigh, Ali. 2017. Ethics: An Indispensable Dimension in the University Rankings. *Science and Engineering Ethics* 23 (1): 65–80. https://doi .org/10.1007/s11948-016-9758-1.

Knowledge Exchange, Cameron Neylon, Rene Belsø, Magchiel Bijsterbosch, Bas Cordewener, Jérôme Foncel, Sascha Friesike, et al. 2019. *Open Scholarship and the Need for Collective Action.* https://doi.org/10.5281/zen odo.3454688.

Kramer, Adam D. I., Jamie E. Guillory, and Jeffrey T. Hancock. 2014. Experimental Evidence of Massive-Scale Emotional Contagion through Social

Networks. *Proceedings of the National Academy of Sciences of the United States of America* 111 (24): 8788–8790. https://doi.org/10.1073/pnas.1320040111.

Krämer, Katrina. 2019. Female Scientists' Pages Keep Disappearing from Wikipedia—What's Going On? *Chemistry World*, July 3. https://www.chem istryworld.com/news/female-scientists-pages-keep-disappearing-from -wikipedia-whats-going-on/3010664.article.

Krieger, Anja. 2016. Germany: Equality or Excellence. *Nature* 537 (7618): S12–S13. https://doi.org/10.1038/537S12a.

Lakoff, George, and Mark Johnson. 1980. *Metaphors We Live By*. Chicago: University of Chicago Press.

Lam, Shyong (Tony) K., Anuradha Uduwage, Zhenhua Dong, Shilad Sen, David R. Musicant, Loren Terveen, and John Riedl. 2011. WP: Clubhouse? An Exploration of Wikipedia's Gender Imbalance. In *Proceedings of the 7th International Symposium on Wikis and Open Collaboration*, 1–10. WikiSym '11. Mountain View, CA: Association for Computing Machinery. https://doi.org/10.1145/2038558.2038560.

Larivière, Vincent, Stefanie Haustein, and Philippe Mongeon. 2015. The Oligopoly of Academic Publishers in the Digital Era. *PLOS ONE* 10 (6): e0127502. https://doi.org/10.1371/journal.pone.0127502.

Larivière, Vincent, and Cassidy R. Sugimoto. 2018. Do Authors Comply When Funders Enforce Open Access to Research? *Nature* 562 (October): 483–486. https://doi.org/10.1038/d41586-018-07101-w.

Larivière, Vincent, Cassidy R. Sugimoto, Benoit Macaluso, Staša Milojević, Blaise Cronin, and Mike Thelwall. 2014. ArXiv E-Prints and the Journal of Record: An Analysis of Roles and Relationships. *Journal of the Association for Information Science and Technology* 65 (6): 1157–1169. https://doi.org/10.1002/asi.23044.

Lebel, Jean, and Robert McLean. 2018. A Better Measure of Research from the Global South. *Nature* 559 (7712): 23–26. https://doi.org/10.1038/d41586 -018-05581-4.

Lee, Carole J., Cassidy R. Sugimoto, Guo Zhang, and Blaise Cronin. 2013. Bias in Peer Review. *Journal of the American Society for Information Science and Technology* 64 (1): 2–17. https://doi.org/10.1002/asi.22784.

Library Publishing Coalition. 2020. Academic and Research Libraries Engaged in Scholarly Publishing. https://librarypublishing.org/.

Lin, Songqing, and Lijuan Zhan. 2014. Trash Journals in China. *Learned Publishing* 27 (2): 145–154. https://doi.org/10.1087/20140208.

Mandela Initiative and Nelson Mandela Foundation. 2017. Dialogues and Workshops. https://mandelainitiative.org.za/dialogues-workshops.html.

Manyika, James, Susan Lund, Jacques Bughin, Jonathan Woetzel, Kalin Stamenov, and Dhruv Dhingra. 2016. Digital Globalization: The New Era of Global Flows. McKinsey Global Institute. https://www.mckinsey.com/business-functions/mckinsey-digital/our-insights/digital-globalization-the-new-era-of-global-flows.

Maracke, Catharina. 2010. Creative Commons International: The International License Porting Project. *Journal of Intellectual Property, Information Technology, and E-commerce Law* 4 (1). http://www.jipitec.eu/issues/jipitec-1-1-2010/2417.

Marginson, Simon. 2019. The Kantian University: Worldwide Triumph and Growing Insecurity. *Australian Universities' Review* 61 (1): 59–70.

Marx, Karl. 1844. "Estranged Labour." In *Economic and Philosophical Manuscripts of 1844*, first manuscript, XXIII. Accessed September 17, 2020. https://www.marxists.org/archive/marx/works/1844/manuscripts/labour.htm.

McCraw, Thomas K. 2007. *Prophet of Innovation: Joseph Schumpeter and Creative Destruction.* Cambridge, MA: Harvard University Press.

Mokyr, Joel. 2009. *The Enlightened Economy: An Economic History of Britain, 1700–1850.* New Haven, CT: Yale University Press.

Mokyr, Joel. 2017. *A Culture of Growth: The Origins of the Modern Economy.* Princeton, NJ: Princeton University Press.

Moore, Samuel. 2017. A Genealogy of Open Access: Negotiations between Openness and Access to Research / Une Généalogie de l'open access: Négociations entre l'ouverture et l'accès à la recherche. *Revue Française des Sciences de l'information et de la communication* 11 (January). https://doi.org/10.4000/rfsic.3220.

Morozov, Evgeny. 2013a. Open and Closed. *New York Times*, March 16, Opinion sec. https://www.nytimes.com/2013/03/17/opinion/sunday/morozov-open-and-closed.html.

Morozov, Evgeny. 2013b. *To Save Everything, Click Here: The Folly of Solutionism.* New York: Public Affairs.

National Institutes of Health. 2015. Plan for Increasing Access to Scientific Publications. https://grants.nih.gov/grants/nih-public-access-plan.pdf.

Neylon, Cameron. 2010. Open Research Computation: An Ordinary Journal with Extraordinary Aims. December 13. https://cameronneylon.net/blog /open-research-computation-an-ordinary-journal-with-extraordinary-aims/.

Neylon, Cameron. 2016. The Complexities of Citation: How Theory Can Support Effective Policy and Implementation. http://repository.jisc.ac.uk /6553/.

Neylon, Cameron. 2017. Case Study: Brazilian Virtual Herbarium. *Research Ideas and Outcomes* 3 (October): e21852. https://doi.org/10.3897/rio.3.e21852.

Neylon, Cameron, Jan Aerts, C. Titus Brown, Simon J. Coles, Les Hatton, Daniel Lemire, K. Jarrod Millman, et al. 2012. Changing Computational Research: The Challenges Ahead. *Source Code for Biology and Medicine* 7 (May): article no. 2. https://doi.org/10.1186/1751-0473-7-2.

Noble, Safiya, and Sarah Roberts. 2019. *Technological Elites, the Meritocracy, and Postracial Myths in Silicon Valley.* https://escholarship.org/uc/item/7z3629nh.

Novak, Mikayla. 2019. Crypto-Friendliness: Understanding Blockchain Public Policy. *Journal of Entrepreneurship and Public Policy.* https://doi.org/10.1108 /JEPP-03-2019-0014.

Olson, Mancur. 1965. *The Logic of Collective Action: Public Goods and the Theory of Groups.* Cambridge, MA: Harvard University Press.

Open Data Charter. n.d. Compiling Data Inventories: Collaborative Working in Action. Accessed January 27, 2021. https://opendatacharter.net.

Organization for Economic Cooperation and Development. 2019.*Global Blockchain Forum—Summary Report.* Geneva: Organization for Economic Cooperation and Development. https://www.oecd.org/finance/2019-OECD -Global-Blockchain-Policy-Forum-Summary-Report.pdf.

Ostrom, Elinor. 1990. *Governing the Commons: The Evolution of Institutions for Collective Action.* Cambridge: Cambridge University Press.

Packer, Abel L., Nicholas Cop, Adriana Luccisano, Amanda Ramalho, and Ernesto Spinak, eds. 2014. SciELO—15 Years of Open Access: An Analytic Study of Open Access and Scholarly Communication. Paris: United Nations Educational, Scientific, and Cultural Organization. https://doi.org/10.7476 /9789230012373.

Page, Scott E. 2008. *The Difference: How the Power of Diversity Creates Better Groups, Firms, Schools, and Societies*. Princeton, NJ: Princeton University Press.

PatientsLikeMe. 2020. https://www.patientslikeme.com/.

Paul Baran. n.d. History-Computer.com. Accessed May 4, 2020. https://history-computer.com/Internet/Birth/Baran.html.

Poppe, Annika Elena, Julia Leininger, and Jonas Wolff. 2019. Introduction: Negotiating the Promotion of Democracy. *Democratization* 26 (5): 759–776. https://doi.org/10.1080/13510347.2019.1593379.

Popper, Karl. 1945. *The Open Society and Its Enemies*. London: Routledge.

Potts, Jason. 2019. *Innovation Commons: The Origin of Economic Growth*. Oxford: Oxford University Press.

Potts, Jason, John Hartley, John Banks, Jean Burgess, Rachel Cobcroft, Stuart Cunningham, and Lucy Montgomery. 2008. Consumer Co-Creation and Situated Creativity. *Industry and Innovation* 15 (5): 459–474.

Prigogine, Ilya, and Isabelle Stengers. 1985. *Order out of Chaos: Man's New Dialogue with Nature*. London: Fontana Press.

Ravetz, Jerome. 1971. *Scientific Knowledge and Its Social Problems*. Oxford: Oxford University Press.

Readings, Bill. 1996. *The University in Ruins*. Cambridge, MA: Harvard University Press.

Ren, Xiang, and Lucy Montgomery. 2015. Open Access and Soft Power: Chinese Voices in International Scholarship. *Media, Culture and Society* 37 (3): 394–408. https://doi.org/10.1177/0163443714567019.

ROARMAP. n.d. Welcome to ROARMAP. Accessed May 4, 2020. http://roarmap.eprints.org/.

Schiermeier, Quirin, and Richard Van Noorden. 2015. Germany Claims Success for Elite Universities Drive. *Nature News* 525 (7568): 168. https://doi.org/10.1038/nature.2015.18312.

Schlosser, Melanie. 2018. Building Capacity for Academy-Owned Publishing through the Library Publishing Coalition. *Library Trends* 67 (2): 359–375. https://doi.org/10.1353/lib.2018.0041.

Schomberg, Rene von, J. Britt Holbrook, Alis Oancea, Shina Caroline Lynn Kamerlin, Ismael Rafois, Merle Jacob, and Paul Wouters. 2019. Indicator

Frameworks for Fostering Open Knowledge Practices in Science and Scholarship. Brussels: European Commission. https://doi.org/10.2777/445286.

Sen, Amartya. 2009. *The Idea of Justice.* Cambridge, MA: Harvard University Press.

Shapin, Steven. 2008. *The Scientific Life: A Moral History of a Late Modern Vocation.* Chicago: University of Chicago Press.

Shirky, Clay. 2015. *Little Rice: Smartphones, Xiaomi, and the Chinese Dream.* New York: Columbia Global Reports.

Smith, Arfon M., Daniel S. Katz, and Kyle E. Niemeyer. 2016. Software Citation Principles. *PeerJ Computer Science* 2 (September): e86. https://doi.org/10.7717/peerj-cs.86.

Software Sustainability Institute. 2015. Software Credit Workshop—Agenda. https://www.software.ac.uk/software-credit/agenda.

Stanford University. 2020. Stanford Facts—Finances. https://facts.stanford.edu/administration/finances/.

Suber, Peter. 2008. The Open Access Mandate at Harvard. *SPARC Open Access Newsletter* 119 (March). https://dash.harvard.edu/bitstream/handle/1/4322574/suber_harvard.html?sequence=1.

Sugimoto, Cassidy R., Nicolas Robinson-Garcia, Dakota S. Murray, Alfredo Yegros-Yegros, Rodrigo Costas, and Vincent Larivière. 2017. Scientists Have Most Impact When They're Free to Move. *Nature News* 550 (7674): 29. https://doi.org/10.1038/550029a.

Swingler, Helen. 2018. SALDRU: Rebooted and on a Mission. University of Capetown News, March 23. http://www.news.uct.ac.za/article/-2018-03-23-saldru-rebooted-and-on-a-mission.

Thunberg, Greta. 2019. *No One Is Too Small to Make a Difference.* London: Penguin Random House.

Tingley, Kim. 2020. Coronavirus Is Forcing Medical Research to Speed Up. *New York Times Magazine,* April 21. https://www.nytimes.com/2020/04/21/magazine/coronavirus-scientific-journals-research.html.

Tsvetkova, Milena, Ruth García-Gavilanes, Luciano Floridi, and Taha Yasseri. 2017. Even Good Bots Fight: The Case of Wikipedia. *PLOS ONE* 12 (2): e0171774. https://doi.org/10.1371/journal.pone.0171774.

Tuhiwai Smith, Linda. 2012. *Decolonizing Methodologies: Research and Indigenous Peoples*. 2nd ed. London: Zed Books.

University of Cambridge. 2020. The University's Mission and Core Values. https://www.cam.ac.uk/about-the-university/how-the-university-and-colleges-work/the-universitys-mission-and-core-values.

ur Rehman, Ikhlaq. 2019. Facebook–Cambridge Analytica Data Harvesting: What You Need to Know. *Library Philosophy and Practice*: 1–11.

Vollmer, Timothy. 2015. It's Time to #MoveFASTR: Support Public Access to Publicly-Funded Research. *Creative Commons* (blog), July 28. https://creativecommons.org/2015/07/28/its-time-to-movefastr-support-public-access-to-publicly-funded-research/.

Wagner, Caroline S., and Koen Jonkers. 2017. Open Countries Have Strong Science. *Nature News* 550 (7674): 32–33. https://doi.org/10.1038/550032a.

Wallis, Todd. 2018. The Rise of Adjunct Faculty: A Brief History. *Inside Scholar*, April 11. https://insidescholar.org/the-rise-of-adjunct-faculty/.

Wikipedia. 2020a. Gender Bias on Wikipedia. Wikipedia. Accessed March 18, 2020. https://en.wikipedia.org/w/index.php?title=Gender_bias_on_Wikipedia&direction=next&oldid=949849258.

Wikipedia. 2020b. Racial Bias on Wikipedia. Wikipedia. Accessed March 3, 2020. https://en.wikipedia.org/w/index.php?title=Racial_bias_on_Wikipedia&oldid=943725321.

Wikipedia. 2020c. List of Wikipedias. Wikipedia. Accessed August 18, 2020. https://en.wikipedia.org/wiki/List_of_Wikipedias.

Wilbanks, John. 2018. Design Issues in E-Consent. *Journal of Law, Medicine and Ethics* 46 (1): 110–118. https://doi.org/10.1177/1073110518766025.

Wilson, Katie, Cameron Neylon, Chloe Brookes-Kenworthy, Richard Hosking, Chun-Kai Huang, Lucy Montgomery, and Alkim Ozaygen. 2019. "Is the Library Open?": Correlating Unaffiliated Access to Academic Libraries with Open Access Support. *LIBER Quarterly* 29 (1): 1–33. https://doi.org/10.18352/lq.10298.

Witschge, Tamara, C. W. Anderson, David Domingo, and Alfred Hermida. 2018. Dealing with the Mess (We Made): Unraveling Hybridity, Normativity, and Complexity in Journalism Studies. *Journalism* 20 (5): 651–659. https://doi.org/10.1177/1464884918760669.

Woolf University. n.d. Discover Woolf. Accessed January 27, 2021. https://woolf.university/.

Worthy, Ben, and Marlen Heide. 2019. Donald Trump: Openness, Secrets and Lies. Democratic Audit UK. February 19. https://www.democraticaudit.com/2019/02/19/donald-trump-openness-secrets-and-lies/.

Wouters, Paul. 2016. *Semiotics and Citations: Theories of Informetrics and Scholarly Communication.* De Gruyter Saur. https://doi.org/10.1515/9783110308464-007.

Further Reading

Arrow, Kenneth. 1962. Economic Welfare and the Allocation of Resources for Innovation. In *The Rate and Direction of Inventive Activity*, edited by Richard Nelson, 609–626. Princeton, NJ: Princeton University Press.

Arthur, W. Brian. 2009. *The Nature of Technology*. New York: Free Press.

Chan, Leslie, and Eve Gray. 2014. Centering the Knowledge Peripheries through Open Access: Implications for Future Research and Discourse on Knowledge for Development. In *Open Development: Networked Innovations in International Development*, edited by Matthew L. Smith and Katherine M. A. Reilly, 197–222. Cambridge, MA: MIT Press.

De Beer, Jeremy, C. J. Armstrong, Chidi Oguamanam, and Tobias Schonwetter. 2014. *Innovation and Intellectual Property: Collaborative Dynamics in Africa*. Cape Town: UCT Press.

Frischmann, Brett M. 2014. *Infrastructure: The Social Value of Shared Resources*. Oxford: Oxford University Press.

Frischmann, Brett M., Michael J. Madison, and Katherine Jo Strandburg. 2014. *Governing Knowledge Commons*. New York: Oxford University Press.

Haeussler, Carolin. 2011. Information-Sharing in Academia and the Industry: A Comparative Study. Special issue, *Research Policy* 40 (1): 105–122. https://doi.org/10.1016/j.respol.2010.08.007.

Harhoff, Dietmar, and Karim R. Lakhani. 2016. *Revolutionizing Innovation Users, Communities, and Open Innovation*. Cambridge, MA: MIT Press.

Hartley, John, and Jason Potts. 2016. *Cultural Science: A Natural History of Stories, Demes, Knowledge and Innovation.* London: Bloomsbury Academic.

Hartley, John, Jason Potts, Lucy Montgomery, Ellie Rennie, and Cameron Neylon. 2019. Do We Need to Move from Communication Technology to User Community? A New Economic Model of the Journal as a Club. *Learned Publishing* 32 (1): 27–35. https://doi.org/10.1002/leap.1228.

Henrich, Joseph. 2016. *The Secret of Our Success.* Princeton, NJ: Princeton University Press.

Hess, Charlotte, and Elinor Ostrom. 2011. *Understanding Knowledge as a Commons: From Theory to Practice.* Cambridge, MA: MIT Press.

Hippel, Eric von. 2006. *Democratizing Innovation.* Cambridge, MA: MIT Press.

Hoggart, Richard. 1992. *An Imagined Life: Life and Times, 1959–91.* London: Chatto and Windus.

Lerner, Josh, and Jean Tirole. 2005. The Economics of Technology Sharing: Open Source and Beyond. *Journal of Economic Perspectives* 19 (2): 99–120. https://doi.org/10.1257/0895330054048678.

Levine, David, and Michele Boldrin. 2008. *Against Intellectual Monopoly.* Cambridge: Cambridge University Press.

Mazzucato, Mariana. 2018. *The Entrepreneurial State: Debunking Public vs. Private Sector Myths.* London: Penguin Books.

Molloy, Jennifer C. 2011. The Open Knowledge Foundation: Open Data Means Better Science. *PLOS Biology* 9 (12): e1001195. https://doi.org/10.1371/journal.pbio.1001195.

Moore, Samuel, Cameron Neylon, Martin Paul Eve, Daniel Paul O'Donnell, and Damian Pattinson. 2017. "Excellence R Us": University Research and the Fetishisation of Excellence. *Palgrave Communications* 3 (1): 1–13. https://doi.org/10.1057/palcomms.2016.105.

Moser, Petra. 2012. Innovation without Patents: Evidence from World's Fairs. *Journal of Law and Economics* 55 (1): 43–74. https://doi.org/10.1086/663631.

Neilsen, Michael. 2011. *Reinventing Discovery: The New Era of Networked Science.* Princeton, NJ: Princeton University Press.

O'Mahony, Siobhán, and Fabrizio Ferraro. 2007. The Emergence of Governance in an Open Source Community. *Academy of Management Journal* 50 (5): 1079–1106. https://doi.org/10.2307/20159914.

Potts, Jason. 2017. Governing the Innovation Commons. *Journal of Institutional Economics* 14 (6): 1025–1047. https://doi.org/10.1017/S1744137417000479.

Royal Society. 2011. *Knowledge, Networks and Nations: Global Scientific Collaboration in the 21st Century.* London: Royal Society.

Slack, Paul. 2014. *The Invention of Improvement: Information and Material Progress in Seventeenth-Century England.* Oxford: Oxford University Press.

Wagner, Caroline S. 2008. *The New Invisible College: Science for Development.* Washington, DC: Brookings Institution Press.

Author Bios

Lucy Montgomery is a professor of knowledge innovation at Curtin University in Australia, where she leads the Innovation in Knowledge Communication research program at the Centre for Culture and Technology. She is also co-lead of the Curtin Open Knowledge Initiative: a major, strategically funded project exploring the possibilities of open knowledge for universities, as well as director of research for Collaborative Open Access Knowledge and Development (COARD). Her work focuses on the ways in which open access and open knowledge are transforming landscapes of knowledge production, sharing, and use.

John Hartley is a John Curtin Distinguished Emeritus Professor at Curtin University and a visiting professor at the London School of Economics and Political Science. His research and publications focus on popular media and culture, journalism, the creative industries, and cultural science. He was founding editor of the *International Journal of Cultural Studies* (1998–2018). Hartley has held executive positions at Cardiff University and Queensland University of Technology, and was an Australian Research Council Federation Fellow (2005–2010).

Cameron Neylon is a professor of research communications at the Centre for Culture and Technology at Curtin University, and director of Collaborative Open Access Research and Development (COARD). He was a founding director of FORCE11, and contributing author to the *Altmetrics Manifesto, Panton Principles for Open Data*, and *Principles for Open Scholarly Infrastructure*. Neylon has been a biochemist and technologist, worked in scholarly publishing as an advocate for open access, and now focuses on studying the changing cultures and institutions of the academy.

Malcolm Gillies is a professor emeritus at the Australian National University and visiting professor at King's College London. During 2007–2014, he was president of City, University of London and London Metropolitan University. He researches and consults in fields of music, education, leadership, and cultural policy.

Eve Gray is a senior research associate in the intellectual property unit at the University of Cape Town. She has had an interest in the disruptive potential of digital publishing since the early 1990s, working as a university press director, academic textbook publishing director, and publishing consultant. Gray is an internationally recognized specialist on open access and the geopolitics of university publishing—an issue that has gained new urgency in the wake of the Rhodes Must Fall student protest movement in 2015 and growing demands for the decolonization of universities in South Africa.

Carsten Herrmann-Pillath is a professor and permanent fellow at the Max Weber Center for Advanced Social and Cultural Studies at the University of Erfurt in Germany. He is an economist, sinologist, and philosopher, and has published widely on issues of cross-disciplinary research, bridging economics, the humanities, and the sciences.

Chun-Kai (Karl) Huang is a senior research fellow (data scientist) in the Centre for Culture and Technology at Curtin University. He has previously worked at the University of Cape Town and University of KwaZulu-Natal. Huang is a mathematical statistician by training, with research interests in statistical modeling, probability theory, financial risk, and more recently, open knowledge.

Joan Leach is a professor and director of the Australian National Centre for the Public Awareness of Science at the Australian National University. She sees firsthand how scientific research thrives in a culture of openness and how mediators like science communicators contribute to the generation of scientific knowledge.

Jason Potts is a professor of institutional economics at RMIT University in Melbourne, where he is the director of the Blockchain Innovation Hub. His research focuses on the economic institutions of innovation.

Xiang Ren is an academic course adviser and senior lecturer in the Australia-China Institute for Arts and Culture at Western Sydney University in Australia. His research revolves around digital publishing, open access, and creative industries in China.

Katherine Skinner is the director of the Educopia Institute, a nonprofit organization in Atlanta, Georgia, that empowers collaborative communities to create, share, and preserve knowledge. Her work includes the cultivation of cross-sector networks (e.g., the Software Preservation Network, MetaArchive Cooperative, BitCurator Consortium, and Library Publishing Coalition) that share expertise and infrastructure across libraries, archives, museums, and publishers, and her research explores the building and sustaining of healthy, diverse knowledge communities.

Cassidy R. Sugimoto is a professor of informatics at the School of Informatics, Computing, and Engineering at Indiana University in Bloomington. She is currently serving as the president of the International Society for Scientometrics and Informetrics. Her research looks at scholarly communication, scientometrics, and science policy.

Katie Wilson is a research fellow in the Centre for Culture and Technology at Curtin University with the Curtin Open Knowledge Initiative project. She has undertaken research in Indigenous education and worked in academic libraries. Her current research focus is on demographic and knowledge diversity as well as access to open knowledge.

Index

Note: page numbers in italics indicate figures and tables.